The Practical
Christian

To order additional copies of *The Practical Christian*,
by Bertram L. Melbourne, call **1-800-765-6955.**

Visit us at **www.reviewandherald.com** for information on other
Review and Herald® products.

The Practical Christian

Christian

MOUTH, MONEY, AND MIND

BERTRAM L. MELBOURNE

REVIEW AND HERALD® PUBLISHING ASSOCIATION
Since 1861 | www.reviewandherald.com

Published by Review and Herald® Publishing Association, Hagerstown, MD 21741-1119

This book was
Edited by Gerald Wheeler
Copyedited by Delma Miller
Cover designed by Ron Pride / Review and Herald® Design Center
Interior designed by Emily Ford / Review and Herald® Design Center
Cover art by Lars Justinen
Typeset: Minion Pro 11/13

PRINTED IN U.S.A.

18 17 16 15 14   5 4 3 2 1

Library of Congress Cataloging-in-Publication Data

Melbourne, Bertram L., 1948-
   The practical Christian : mouth, money, mind, and more [2Q14] / Bertram L. Melbourne.
      pages cm
   Includes bibliographical references.
   ISBN 978-0-8280-2707-6
   1. Bible. James--Criticism, interpretation, etc. I. Title.
   BS2785.52.M45 2014
   227'.9106--dc23

                          20130115351

ISBN 978-0-8280-2707-6

Dedication

To those who disciple me,
and to those who benefited from
that relationship
with me!

Acknowledgments

To my family members who encouraged me in this task and endured by long periods of silence and noninteraction, my tremendous gratitude!

To those who encouraged me and prayed for my successful completion of the task, my profound thanks.

To those who read and edited the manuscript, a big thank-you!

To Veronica Clarke-Tasker for her willingness to be "guinea pig" and explore the material in a class and for giving her encouragement and suggestions, I say thanks!

Contents

INTRODUCTION

Several years ago Robert Johnston recommended and encouraged me to study the book of James for my doctoral thesis. Because of not controlling my tongue, as the book teaches, I lost that opportunity and wrote instead on another fascinating topic—discipleship. It gave me a new perspective on Jesus, His disciples, us, and the work to which He committed us.

But the current assignment from the Review and Herald Publishing Association gave me the unique opportunity not only to do in-depth work on the book of James but to do so through the lens of discipleship. Scholars see its author as giving exhortations to believers, and that is certainly true. Yet I would press that conclusion to another level by asking, Exhortation to what intent or for what purpose? The author certainly had an objective in mind. What was it? I presume most scholars would agree that it was to have his readers become better Christians.

Now, if we accept this premise, then we could further ask, Who is a Christian? A Christian is a follower of Jesus. The invitation He issued to His first disciples was "Follow Me." They heard this as "Become My disciple," and that is what they did. Jesus' final commission to them on the mount in Galilee was to go disciple others (Matt. 28:19). Luke tells how Saul of Tarsus went to Damascus to find those belonging to "the Way" so that he could persecute them. The Way refers to the path of discipleship. The Gospel writer also tells us that believers first received the name Christians—imitators of Jesus—at Antioch, where Barnabas and Saul had preached Jesus very effectively. We could therefore conclude that a Christian is one who follows, obeys, and imitates Jesus. It seems that, given the nature of the material in the book of James, this is what the author intended. We will therefore examine the book to see what he said to his readers that would advance their commitment to, following of, and advocacy for their Lord.

Viewed through these lenses, some fascinating themes emerge, and thus I invite your careful attention. While most go to James for discussion of faith and works and/or poverty and wealth, the book has far more substance. It teems with intriguing ideas and topics. They include: discipleship of the tongue; discipleship of the pocketbook; and discipleship of the mind. The author seemed to have been very passionate on some of those issues, and some of them he even repeats several times in his short work. It suggests they may have not only been important but especially significant to his readers. As a result we need to see what he says on such issues. Yet they are not the only ones that he addressed. He spends time on the purpose of trials and its role in the Christian life. The same is true for favoritism. Two significant, and possibly unique, discussions concern the role of desire in sin and how to root it out, as well as how to treat the disconnect between words and deeds/profession and practice.

I invite you to an adventure that will deepen your faith; enrich your experience; brighten your life; harness your tongue; open your pocketbook in a good way; free your mind; remove your fears; curb your desires; and unleash the potential of prayer. And remember, you never get more out of anything than you put into it. So give the study of James your best shot. You will not be disappointed. And, of course, share what you gain with another, and perhaps you may succeed in reclaiming a lost spiritual brother or sister. May God bless and guide your adventure and encounter with the Word.

CHAPTER 1

James: From Unbelieving Brother to Committed Follower, Leader, and Advocate

The book of James is a brief but captivating book. Although it opens with a salutation that names the sender and the recipients, yet a problem still persists. Who is the charmer behind it? While the author identifies himself as James, several different individuals in Jesus' circle bore that name—James the son of Zebedee (Matt. 4:21; Mark 1:19; Luke 5:10), James the son of Alphaeus (Matt. 10:3; Mark 3:18; Luke 6:15), James the brother of Jesus (Matt. 13:55; Mark 6:3), and James the father of Judas (Luke 6:16). Some identify a fifth James—the son of a Mary who was present at the Crucifixion; he had a brother named Joses. Zebedee's son couldn't be the author, for he was martyred early. Neither could the second, since we know little beyond mention of his name in the lists. The father of Judas is improbable if not impossible, and the fifth is questionable, since some scholars associate him with the third, while others disagree, wondering why Scripture would identify his mother through him instead of as the mother of Jesus.[1]

This leaves the third James—the brother of our Lord. Some scholars believe he is the author of the epistle, while others credit it to an unknown second-century disciple. If we view the Lord's brother as author, we still must answer some significant questions, such as Was he a follower of Jesus? If so, why don't we have record of his activities with Him? If not, when did he become a Christian? In essence the issue becomes one of how he moved from unbelieving brother to committed follower, leader, and advocate.

Jesus and His Family Members

The relationship between Jesus and His family is fascinating. When He was 12, His mother and earthly father lost him for four days in Jerusalem despite knowing the authorities had tried to kill Him at birth. At a wedding in Cana of Galilee His mother sought to "show Him off" prior to His own readiness to display His miracle-working prowess. A proud mother and caring relative, her primary motive may have concerned averting a family embarrassment because of the absence of the wine so integral to wedding festivities at the time. So she volunteered Him. His answer, "What is that to you and to Me, woman? My hour has not yet come," while not disrespectful then, is strange to us today. It reveals Jesus' passion to be faithful to His mission and His Father's timing.

During His Galilean ministry the crowds flocked Jesus. He was so overworked that He had no time to eat. Hearing His dilemma, His family members tried at least twice to intervene. First, they walked 30 miles to Capernaum to restrain Him, believing His actions proved Him crazy (see Mark 3:21). Second, they sought to talk to Him, perhaps with the intention of convincing Him to return home (see Matt. 12:46ff.). The Mark passage is interesting. The KJV translates it "his friends." However, the Greek idiom, according to A. T. Robertson, "most likely means the kinspeople or family of Jesus as is common in the LXX [Septuagint]."[2] Moreover, he thinks that since verse 31 specifically names Jesus' mother and brothers, they are the friends in verse 21.[3] The Matthew passage shows their disrespect for Him and His mission.

What is evident is that His family members were not with Him. They neither accepted His mission nor joined His followers. His response that His disciples were His mother and brother and sister, when told that His mother and brothers were outside seeking Him, meant He didn't count them among His followers. Besides, the fact that they came to get Him indicated that they didn't accept Him either. Doubtless it included James. Still other telling incidents involving James lead us to believe he was an unbelieving brother up to the very end.

Jesus and James

John records an interesting incident with his siblings that may have occurred around the fall of A.D. 30.[4] After observing that Jesus was purposely staying away from Judea because the Jews there wanted to kill Him, he notes that as the Feast of Tabernacles approached, Jesus' brothers went to Him with the counsel: "Depart from here and go into Judea, that Your disciples also may see the works that You are doing. For no one does anything in secret while he himself seeks to be known openly. If You do these things, show Yourself to the world" (John 7:3, 4). Again it would include James, since the passage does not give a different opinion for him.

At worst the words were mean and sarcastic. At best they were disingenuous. If James and his brothers knew the Jews wanted to kill Jesus, were they sending him to His death? Were they directing Him to make a public show so as to be in conflict with the authorities? If they were loving, devoted siblings, would they have even offered such advice? Reading between the lines, one could detect some jealousy and disloyalty. Also, it appears they are older than He, for they try to dictate His actions, which they may not have attempted, especially in their culture, if He were an elder brother. Ellen White agrees that they are older and suggests that His words and actions often displeased them as they unsuccessfully tried to control Him.[5] This supports the view that they were older children of Joseph from an earlier marriage. They reveal they are devout Jews by going up to Jerusalem for the feast. Ellen White believed that they were torn between the stature of the Jewish authorities and the devout life they had witnessed in their brother.[6] Nevertheless, their reaction confirms their faith in Judaism. Anyway, why would they even make such a suggestion to Jesus? John does not leave us in doubt: "For even His brothers did not believe in Him" (verse 5). Again, it would include James. As late as the fall of A.D. 30 James and his siblings were still unbelievers. When did he become a Christian?

A poignant family moment for Jesus occurs at Calvary. As He hangs on the cross facing physical and emotional pain while staring at death, His last thoughts were about neither Himself nor His suffering. Rather, He was concerned about His mother and her pain. Though she had not openly accepted His mission, she was still His mother. He was dying, and typically sons bury their mothers, not mothers their sons. Yet this was to be her lot, so He thought of her future in a culture that judged a woman's worth by the men in her life. Her husband was dead, He was dying, and she would be at the mercy of a cruel society. It was for this very reason He had raised the widow of Nain's son to life. But why such a concern at all? Didn't He have brothers whom society would expect to care for her?

As Jesus thought about His mother's welfare, it is significant that He did not entrust her to His brothers. He had reasons. At least two things are evident. First, if Mary was their mother, there would be no need for Him to consider her welfare after His departure. She would naturally fall under their protection. That He had to think about her life after His death might indicate they were not her children. Some believe they were, in fact, Mary's stepsons and His half brothers as sons of Joseph from an earlier marriage.[7] That He entrusted her to John, His best friend and perhaps a cousin,[8] is fascinating.

A second point about the brothers of Jesus that could be significant is their absence at the cross. Devout Jews, they went to the A.D. 30 Passover when Jesus said He would not go (John 7:8-10). Could it be they did not want to identify with Him given their status in Judaism? Is it possible that Jesus did not commit Mary to their care because He could not guarantee her well-being, since they had not accepted His mission? At any rate, what is evident is that up to the point of His death they are not numbered among His followers and not considered trustworthy enough to provide for Mary after Jesus' departure. It means that James is still an unbelieving brother of Jesus. When did he come to faith?

The Conversion of James

Thus the Gospels close with a negative perspective of James. Yet what a complete reversal we experience when we read the book of Acts. It lists James among those in the upper room who obediently awaited Jesus' last promise before His ascension—the power that would accompany the receipt of the Spirit (Acts 1:12-14). He is therefore one of those upon whom the Spirit fell on the day of Pentecost (Acts 2:1-3). Later we see him as chair for the first Christian council (Acts 15) and as the author of a New Testament epistle. What caused such a dramatic turn of events?

As I suggest elsewhere, the disciples reflect a similar portrait.[9] At the close of the Gospels they have a very poor image. They all forsook Jesus and fled at the arrest. Judas betrayed Him. Peter denied Him. They watched the Crucifixion from afar, if present at all—John being the possible exception (John 19:26). Nor did they request His body or were present at His burial. Instead, the women and two heretofore uncommitted disciples ensured an honorable burial. The disciples went into hiding after the Crucifixion, fearing the Jews (John 20:19). The women discovered the empty tomb and first encountered the resurrected Lord.

Yet in the book of Acts we see those same disciples boldly proclaiming the gospel. Peter fearlessly accused the Jews of killing Jesus. He has faith strong enough to work miracles and defy the authorities. We see those supposed cowards now allowing themselves to be beaten, imprisoned, and even killed for the cause of Christ. Everywhere they boldly witness to their faith. Peter even tells others, "We did not follow cunningly devised fables when we made known to you the power and coming of our Lord Jesus Christ, but were eyewitnesses of His majesty" (2 Peter 1:16). What was responsible for such a tremendous change?

Again, as pointed out elsewhere, each encounter that one had with the resurrected Lord was a life-changing, transformational experience. Scripture declares that after each incident they remembered His words. It means each time they saw Him—seeing and hearing came together—they finally understood His mission. With illumination came transformation.[10] The same happened to Saul of Tarsus. On the Damascus road he had a personal visit from the resurrected Lord (the implication of the word usage in 1 Corinthians 15:1-9, which employs the same word for all the appearances). When he saw and heard the Lord, seeing and hearing came together and comprehension occurred. The life-transforming change took him from the gospel's leading persecutor and archenemy to its chief advocate and foremost proponent. Did James and the other family members have a similar experience?

It is an intriguing question that needs exploration. While we know neither the precise time nor the details of James's conversion or that of the rest of the family, Scripture does tell us that Jesus "was buried, and that he rose again the third day . . . : and that he was seen of Cephas, then of the twelve: after that, he was seen of above five hundred brethren at once. . . . *After that, he was seen of James;* then of all the apostles" (verses 4-7, KJV). Commenting on the passage, Robertson observes that it explains the presence of Jesus' brothers in the upper room.[11] Barclay concludes that this James is beyond doubt Jesus' brother.[12] The consensus is that Jesus' appearance to James led to his final conversion. If so, then it is consistent with the notion that every appearance produced an illumination that resulted in transformation and commitment. It remains that many still need an encounter with the resurrected Lord so that they can experience such illumination and transformation.

It seems the appearances of Jesus moved His mother and siblings from unbelievers to supporters. So James's encounter shifted him from unbelieving brother to committed follower. Once converted, he appears to have contributed significantly to the neophyte church, though he didn't seem to have received deference as a brother of Jesus. Interestingly, though present for the replacement of Judas, Scripture does not mention his name. As a recent convert, he did not meet the criteria outlined by Peter. He was not one of those who were "with us the whole time the Lord Jesus was living among us, beginning from John's baptism to the time when Jesus was taken up from us" (Acts 1:21, 22, NIV).

We conclude that since he was in the group who obediently stayed in the upper room until the fulfillment of the promise of the Holy Spirit, he was among those who got the gift of the Spirit and who spoke in tongues at Pentecost. Though not listed among those chosen to resolve the issue between the Hebraic and the Hellenistic Jews, he did rise in the leadership of the church. Some scholars see him as head of the church in Jerusalem. By the time of the first Christian council (Acts 15) we see him as its chair. He facilitated the meeting, gave a summary of the discussion, and proposed a resolution to the issue. The fact that everyone agreed with his proposals confirms his leadership abilities and conflict resolution skills.

Paul seemed to have had great respect for and excellent relations with James (Acts 15; 21:18; Gal. 1:19; 2:9). It appears that each time the apostle went to Jerusalem he met with James. In addition, Paul calls him, along with Peter and John, "pillars of the church" (see Gal. 2:9). To understand this reference fully, we must note that the rabbis referred to Abraham as a pillar of the world. Contemporaries also used the word in reference to Moses and the righteous.[13] James, Peter, and John are pillars, since they are the main leaders of the Jerusalem church.[14] Thus we see that while not accepting Jesus from the beginning of His ministry, James rose from unbelieving brother to committed follower to pillar of the church in a relatively short time. He even came to be called "James the Just" and a model disciple.[15] Both non-Christian and Christian residents of Jerusalem respected him for his piety. After procurator Festus died about the year A.D. 62, Ananus II, the high priest, executed James. It brought such a public outcry that the new procurator deposed Ananus from office.[16] What we see here is the amazing, transforming power of the gospel. It does change lives, and no one is beyond the scope of its reach.

James the Author

Yet that does not seem to be all the information about James in the New Testament. He appears to have also become a Christian author. Some scholars attribute the epistle bearing the name James to his pen. While not giving the specifics of his identity, the author refers to himself as "James, a servant of God and of the Lord Jesus Christ" (James 1:1, KJV). It is an interesting contrast to Paul, who usually identifies himself as a servant of Jesus Christ. In fact, James is unique in that he is the only New Testament author using the attribution "servant" who links it to God, not to Jesus (Titus 1:1 being a possible exception in which Paul makes a similar reference). Is it possible, given the nature of some of what will follow, especially in regard to faith and works, that James sets a contrast from the opening line of his epistle? Moreover, if we see here the hand of James the Just, this suggests fairness, fair play, balance, and a stand for justice. As a leader of the Jerusalem church that had a passion for the Judaic roots of Christianity, he could be seeking a balance that he may have achieved by identifying himself as a servant of both Father and Son.

While some in the early church referred to James as an apostle, it's notable that he does not, but instead calls himself a servant of God and Jesus. It speaks to his humility, a notion also seen in the fact that while he could claim relationship to the Lord and present himself as Jesus' brother, he did not. Also, while he may have identified himself as a leader of the Jerusalem church and/or chair of the first Christian council, he again didn't. No wonder his piety became reputed and no doubt contributed to the great respect the early Christians had for him. Despite his achievements, he calls himself a slave, which means that he is the property of God and Christ and thus at Their service to do Their bidding. We can learn much here! Ecclesiastical titles are important and denote office, but are subservient to Christian brotherhood, service, and servant leadership. Titles may confer honor and privileges, but there is no greater privilege than the opportunity to serve the Father, the Son, and Their people on earth. "Our Savior declared John the Baptist to be the greatest of the prophets; yet when asked if he were the Christ, John declared himself unworthy even to unloose his Master's sandals. When his disciples came with the complaint that all men were turning to the new teacher, John reminded them that he was but the forerunner of the Coming One. Workers with this spirit are needed today."[17]

James realized that in working with and for the church, he was doing the same with and for its founder and His Father. Thus he was himself in a servant relationship with Them. We do not truly begin to experience the joys of the Christian life until we realize that we find the greatest freedom on earth in enslavement to Jesus Christ. It is a great but true paradox and a reality that we can't understand until it is experienced. Not only James but many other leaders and people in the early church discovered its truth. Many in the modern church can have that joy too if they will join in the relationship that James had with Father and Son.

Nature of the Epistle/Epistles

Because the epistle addresses itself to the 12 tribes scattered among the nations, we regard it as one of the catholic or general epistles. The designation is so wide-ranging that it is impossible to identify a specific location or region. It could include descendants of any Diaspora who did not return home, whether they lived in Rome, Egypt, Babylonia, or other parts of the Roman Empire. But doubtlessly it especially referenced those who scattered in the Diaspora that followed Stephen's death and the ensuing persecution by Saul of Tarsus. Yet we can deduce a few things from this description. First, it identifies both the author and the recipients as Jews. Other words used in the epistle also support such an interpretation. Second, the designation identifies the receivers as Diaspora Jews, i.e., Jews not resident in Palestine but who instead lived in Hellenistic lands. It suggests that James wrote the epistle for Jewish Christians in such regions but not excluding non-Christian Jews. Such a concern and perspective would not be inimical to James the Just as the leader of the Jerusalem church.

Ancient letters had four general sections: *prescript*—identifying sender, recipients, and giving general greetings; *proem*—giving thanksgiving and petition to God as well as wishes for the health of the receivers; *body*—conveying the main message; and the *eschatokoll*—carrying benedictory wishes in the sender's own hand, corresponding to the modern signature.18 James begins with a prescript (James 1:1) and races to the body with no proem. The body extends from verse 2 through James 5:18. It closes without an eschatokoll but with a final exhortation.

Some scholars see James as one of the earliest New Testament documents. Others view it as late, dating to the second century. Given the primitive nature of its theology and failure to mention significant events such as the emergence of Gentile Christianity and Paul's problems after the Jerusalem Council, an early date seems advisable.[19] I go with scholars who date it between A.D. 45 and 48.

The book has no central motif but a number of themes. It comes from the heart of a pastor designed to exhort the flock to fruitful and productive living. Since James is writing to individuals who may have faced persecution, it is understandable that faith is a major element of the epistle. He writes to strengthen faith, but primarily in terms of its lived impact.

A second major theme is good works. James had a problem with those who profess faith but did not let it regulate their behavior. He sees good deeds as the fruit of faith. The so-called conflict between James and Paul about the role of faith and works is in fact a nonstarter if indeed James wrote his book as early as we believe. The apostle would have finished his epistle before Paul began writing generally, and Romans, Galatians, and

Ephesians specifically. What we have are two differing approaches aimed at the same target—helping people to understand the role of faith and works in the Christian life. James, on the one hand, emphasizes the positive role of works in validating faith in light of the Master's statement "By their fruits ye shall know them" (Matt. 7:16, ASV). Paul, on the other hand, given his pharisaic background and intimate acquaintance with and knowledge of Judaism's works orientation, emphasized salvation by faith. Both, however, knew and understood the role of the opposite grace in real Christian life. Thus it is folly to pit one against the other. They are, in fact, complementary, since genuine faith manifests itself through lived, practicing deeds.

Other themes of the book include control of the tongue, partiality, wisdom, prayer, and the roles of wealth, justice, and Christian piety. Written as exhortations or as part of a sermon, the epistle touches on several elements of the gospel and church doctrines. One can readily see the importance for faith as well as James's passion for Christian faithfulness. In fact, he does spend time bridging the disconnect between walk and talk and between profession and practice. Finally, some scholars detect closeness, if not similarities, between the epistle and the Sermon on the Mount, especially the Beatitudes. We do indeed find some similarities and can easily explain them since, while James did not become a disciple during Jesus' ministry, he may have listened to some of His teaching. Thus the Holy Spirit would have brought back to his memory those things especially beneficial both to his community and for future generations. Read with an open mind, and test those similarities.

Summary

We have taken a slight glimpse of the spiritual journey of James as he moved from nonbeliever to believer and committed follower who played a leadership role in the church, adjudicating difficult situations; living a pious life; mentoring and ministering to others through his life and written word; and eventually paying the ultimate price with his life. In the next few pages, we will look at the counsels he gave and see what they have to say for Christian life in the twenty-first century. We are out for a great adventure!

---

[1] See Siegfried H. Horn, ed., *Seventh-day Adventist Bible Dictionary*, rev. ed. (Washington, D.C.: Review and Herald Pub. Assn., 1979), pp. 548, 549.

[2] A. T. Robertson, *Word Pictures in the New Testament* (Grand Rapids: Baker Book House, 1930), vol. 1, p. 281.

[3] *Ibid.*

[4] Francis D. Nichol, ed., *The Seventh-day Adventist Bible Commentary* (Hagerstown, Md.: Review and Herald Pub. Assn., 1953-1957, 1980), vol. 5, p. 231.

[5] Ellen G. White, *The Desire of Ages* (Mountain View, Calif.: Pacific Press Pub. Assn., 1898), pp. 87, 88.

[6] *Ibid.,* pp. 450, 451.

[7] See *The SDA Bible Commentary,* vol. 5, p. 282.

[8] Deduced from a comparison of John 19:25, Matthew 27:56, and Mark 15:40. Cf. David Noel Freedman, ed., *The Anchor Bible Dictionary* (New York: Doubleday, 1992), vol. 3, p. 620.

[9] See Bertram L. Melbourne, *Slow to Understand: The Disciples in Synoptic Perspective* (Lanham, Md.: University Press of America, 1988).

[10] *Ibid.*

[11] Robertson, vol. 4, p. 188.

[12] William Barclay, *The Letters to the Corinthians,* rev. ed. (Philadelphia: Westminster Press, 1975), p. 144.

[13] Ulrich Wilckens, *"stulos,"* in Gerhard Kittel and Gerhard Friedrich, eds., *Theological Dictionary of the New Testament* (Grand Rapids: Wm. B. Eerdmans Pub. Co., 1971), vol. 7, p. 734.

[14] *Ibid.*

[15] Ralph P. Martin and Peter H. Davids, eds., *Dictionary of the Later New Testament and Its Developments* (Downers Grove, Ill.: InterVarsity Press, 1997), pp. 546, 547.

[16] Craig S. Keener, *The IVP Bible Background Commentary: New Testament* (Downers Grove, Ill.: InterVarsity Academic Press, 1993), p. 687.

[17] Ellen G. White, *Gospel Workers* (Washington, D.C.: Review and Herald Pub. Assn., 1915), p. 143.

[18] Cf. Werner G. Kümmel, *Introduction to the New Testament,* trans. Howard Clark Kee, rev. English ed. (Nashville: Abingdon, 1975), pp. 248, 249.

[19] Robertson, vol. 6, pp. 4, 5. Cf. Keener, pp. 686, 687; Bruce Metzger, *The New Testament: Its Background, Growth, and Content* (Nashville: Abingdon, 1982), pp. 252, 253. For a contrary view, see Kümmel, pp. 401-403.

CHAPTER 2

The Purpose of Trials

James 1:2-12 is part of a section in which the author seems to be giving encouragement on how to live through difficult and trying times. If James wrote this epistle as early as we believe, it offered great comfort to Christians dispersed by the persecution Saul of Tarsus initiated after Stephen's stoning, and to new believers facing hardship for their acceptance of Jesus as Lord. However, his message applies to Christians of all ages, since everyone needs to understand the purpose of trials and how to endure their relentless attack and severe pressures.

James begins the body of his letter by addressing his readers as "my brethren." Though a masculine word, it is inclusive. Such an engaging introduction would immediately build rapport and engender feelings of friendship, mutuality, and fellowship. The word "brethren" stresses the bond of affection that was and is still shared by those belonging to the Christian community. Belonging to God's household, we are joint heirs with Jesus, and thus family (Rom. 8:17). Jesus isn't ashamed to call us brethren (Heb. 2:11, 12), and we must reciprocate with fellow Christians. We should not take such a tie lightly. For some it runs deeper than blood relationships, but all should cherish it. James appeals to this sense of camaraderie and family to identify with his readers. The "my" even brings the fellowship closer and suggests a deeper bonding. On the basis of this established interrelationship he proceeds to present the purpose of trials in the Christian life.

The Purpose of Trials

James invites Christians to have the right attitude toward trials and temptations. He enjoins his readers to consider it all joy, whole joy, unmixed joy,[1] even pure joy,[2] to suffer. How can we possibly regard events and circumstances that create grief, distraction, suffering, pain, and even destroy faith as things of joy? Yet James goes even further: "Consider it pure joy . . . whenever . . ." (James 1:2, NIV). This suggests it is not a matter of if the Christian will suffer persecution but rather when. It will occur, and is just a matter of what form such trial will take. To convey his thought, James used an indefinite temporal conjunction[3] in Greek. It literally means "whenever" and further serves to underline the notion of the certainty of temptation. Why does he view persecution with such certainty?

The issue goes to the heart of Christian life. Committed Christians exasperate the devil. He will do anything to distract and/or breach their relationship with God. Trials and temptations are among the tools he employs. If we do not experience difficulties and trials, it could indicate that the devil is content with us. That does not mean we should invite temptations. Yet we should be happy when we face them—they tell us we are doing something right and we've attracted the enemy's attention. That is why the Christian can consider facing temptations a joy. But what does that really mean? How can we view temptation from such a perspective?

And with what grace should Christians face temptations? James says joy. He does not refer to a superficial attitude or a plastic, unmeaning smile. True joy has its source deep inside. To grasp it, we should recognize that the word used here often appears in the greeting of letters, especially Christian epistles, and can mean rejoicing. Loh and Hatton think a great way to see what James is saying here is to render it "Consider yourselves fortunate," or "You must understand that it is beneficial for you . . ." or "You must feel great satisfaction when . . ."[4] They conclude that "it is significant that the readers are commanded to have a sense of happiness and joy, or even 'satisfaction,' in face of trials." Though opposition and trials may come from without, it is a quality from within that determines a true genuine response consistent with our profession of faith in Jesus Christ. It is an attitude of fortitude, forgiveness, rejoicing, peace, and calm that relies on God despite the external circumstances.

Such faith does not diminish or bend under pressure but relies completely on God. It has its origin in a secure relationship with Jesus and acknowledges God as friend. Christians with such an attitude of trust can thereby turn their lives over to God, no matter what may happen around them or come their way. They cease reliance on self—the essence of a sinful way of life—and replace anxiety, fear, fret, cares, and worry (self-control) with rejoicing, joy, peace, and hope—Christ-control and the essence of a Christian way of life. At its core, this is what Christian living entails. It is trustful reliance on God. Paul describes such an experience in Romans 8:35-39, from which he says nothing can separate us.

One can find New Testament examples that illustrate such an outlook. First, it is the mind-set that motivated Jesus to pray on behalf of His persecutors at the cross. Second, it is the quality that allowed Peter to rejoice when suffering for his Lord and could make him sleep so soundly and peacefully on the night before his impending execution that it took an angel to awaken him (Acts 12). Third, it is the outlook that motivated Paul to write Philippians with such joy and rejoicing despite wrongful imprisonment and related suffering. Fourth, it is the kind of approach that made members of the early church rejoice at being counted worthy to suffer like and for their Lord. It is the stance that says if my Lord had to suffer to save me, I can endure suffering for His sake. Such attitude and circumstance motivated James to exhort Christians to count it all joy when called on to face trials and temptations of varied kinds.

That James invites Christians to count or consider it joy suggests other options are possible. It means that Christians have a choice in the matter of how they view temptation. Like the proverbial illustration of whether the glass is half full or half empty, it is simply a matter of perspective. Some seem wired to regard things from the negative, while others focus on the positive. James invites Christians to choose a positive outlook on suffering. Even if the enemy and his cohorts designed temptation for harm, Christians can and must disappoint them by viewing it positively and thereby rejoice.

Where did James get such an outlook? Jesus said in a beatitude, "Blessed are those who are persecuted for righteousness' sake. . . . Blessed are you when they revile and persecute you, and say all kinds of evil against you" (Matt. 5:10, 11). He admonished His disciples, "Rejoice and be exceedingly glad," when faced with temptation (verse 12). James is mirroring the concepts of his Master. While he had not yet accepted his brother as Messiah, he may have heard the Sermon on the Mount and the characteristics for citizenship in the divine kingdom. They must have made a lasting impression on him. Having borne fruit in his own life, he now employed them to inspire and motivate others. That is why we should never write off anyone as hopeless. Whereas Jesus used the verb "to rejoice" in the imperative, James used the cognate noun with the imperative of the verb "to count" or "consider." Here is one instance in which James shows similarity with the Sermon on the Mount. And, as we shall see, we must regard trials in a similar way, because of the good results that can emanate from them—the strong Christian qualities they can produce.

James's description of Christians' encounters with temptation is revealing. He says that they "fall" into it. He uses a compound word found only here in the New Testament but which Thucydides used to mean "falling into affliction."[5] Literally translated, it means "to fall around" and is "the picture of being surrounded by trials."[6] Thus James declares that it is neither unique nor unusual for Christians to find themselves encircled by temptation. Yet some Christians lose heart and others their faith when they encounter trials. Perhaps we do not all understand what the Christian life entails and how much help is available.

It amazes me how Christians walk around puny and powerless when the same awesome power that raised Jesus from the dead is available to us. To describe such power, Paul exhausted all the Greek words available for it, piling them on top of each other (Eph. 1:18-20). Why then do we seem so impotent? One day I saw 180-pound Joe lift a 230-pound man with just one hand and then move him around. Noting our amazement, Joe said, "There is nothing as impotent as a man who does not know his strength." The same is true of Christians and the church.

The kind of temptation James says that Christians will face fascinates me. He calls it "divers temptations" (James 1:2, KJV). The Greek word is revealing. Robertson translates it "manifold" and says its basic meaning is "variegated" or "many-colored."[7] It indicates that temptations are not of one stripe or variety. Rather, they are multifaceted and multidimensional. If temptations are of this nature and quality, what should be the Christian's attitude toward them?

Before answering this question, it's important next to examine the implications of the word James used for temptation. Some commentators believe it relates primarily to external trials, since it can also mean "testing" and can refer to a bird testing its wings or of God testing Abraham to see if he would offer Isaac as a sacrifice or to the queen of Sheba testing the wisdom of Solomon.[8] Mayor concurs and identifies the persecution following Stephen's martyrdom, the martyrdom of James, and Paul's depiction of his own sufferings (1 Cor. 4:9ff. and 2 Cor. 11:23ff.) as examples.[9] One can define the word as "anything that tries or tests faith or character." James uses *peirasmoi*, which implies "far more than the word 'temptations' conveys to the modern English reader. It includes such afflictions as sickness, persecution, poverty, and calamity, as well as direct enticements to sin. Trials, whether expressly designed by Satan to tempt a man to sin, or only to annoy and harass him, are always a test of Christian experience"[10] The nature of the word allows it to cover both internal temptations and external tests. The primary focus here may be the latter. It envisions the trials, tests, persecutions, hardships, and difficulties that often afflict the Christian path.

Before we go any further we need to examine something about trials and temptations. To do so, let's use the body to illustrate. We know there's good stress (eustress) and bad stress (distress). The body, however, does not discriminate between them. Stress is not the problem. What is problematic is how we react to stress and how often we create stressful situations for the body. The body can and does cope with stress, but sustained hyperactivity, along with worry, keeps the body in a stress mode. It produces chemicals that in sustained levels harm the body. Likewise, we have good temptations and bad temptations. Temptations in and of themselves are harmless until and unless we yield to them. Remember, sin lies in yielding to temptation. It is how we face them and what we do with them that is harmful. To Christians, all temptations—good or bad—must be approached from the same joyful perspective.

Besides, temptations can be internal or external. Internal temptations affect the individual and his or her own thoughts, feelings, and motives. External trials involve others and the challenges and/or problems brought to bear upon another. For James, external temptations should produce an attitude of rejoicing. Why? Christians should count themselves worthy and privileged to join [their] Lord in suffering for the sake of the gospel. Yet the apostle offers still other reasons for this kind of attitude and fortitude toward facing trials. You see, Christians should know that "the testing of [their] faith produces patience" (James 1:3). The word for "knowing" implies knowledge gained through experience. I often say to my students and parishioners that some of us do not know how to pray or can't recognize answers to our prayers. For example, when we pray for patience and the Lord sends the trials that are the agents for generating the patience we want, we complain. But that doesn't make a lot of sense. The only way to gain experience and develop patience from trials and temptations is to successfully endure them. I hear someone saying that even if you do not successfully endure trials, you still gain knowledge. I agree but must admit that we do not acquire endurance and patience until we have attained success.

James supports such a view himself when he mentions the testing of faith. His choice of words makes his meaning unmistakable. Robertson notes, "The use of *to dokimion* (neuter article with neuter single adjective) here and in 1 Pet. 1:7, clearly means 'the genuine element in your faith,' not 'crucible' nor 'proving.' Your faith like gold stands the test of fire and is approved as standard."[11] The apostle emphasizes not the process of testing but the result—the refined product produced after success is achieved. Please also note that it is the testing of faith that brings this about. Faith infers trust and reliance on God—the ability to turn the life completely over to Him in a trusting relationship, knowing that with Him you are in the safest of hands. Those who can face trials and temptations from this perspective will come through with patience as overcomers.

Yet what is patience? The Greek word James uses is a compound one. It comprises a preposition meaning "under" and a verb meaning "to remain" or "to abide." Thus patience is the ability to abide/endure under. Under what? is a good question. The answer based on James 1:3 is trials and temptations. In the context of James 1, patience is the end result of endurance under such trials and temptations. Thus it is a discipline designed to produce strength, reliance, and connection with God.

James goes one step further when he exhorts his readers to let patience have its perfect work. It is a call to endure under the refining fires of persecution and to let it have its designed end. The apostle calls it "its perfect work" (verse 4). The word used, *telois*, means "end," "completion," or "maturity." Thus James advises that Christians allow trials to go to their designed aim and complete their intended end, which is the development of a mature Christian character in individual believers. Such advice is essential, for it isn't easy to endure under trials, and some tend to give up or give in. Christians must stay the course and hold on no matter what transpires or comes their way.

So what is the purpose of trials and temptations? From the above we can conclude that trials provide growth opportunities on a faith adventure. God intends them to assist Christians in developing spiritual strength, stamina, and endurance. James says it best: "That you may be perfect and complete, lacking nothing" (verse 4). His conclusion appears in James 1:12 and pronounces a beatitude on those who endure trials and temptations: "Blessed is the man who endures temptation; for when he has been approved, he will receive the crown of life which the Lord has promised to those who love Him." It is close to Jesus' "Blessed are those who are persecuted for righteousness' sake, for theirs is the kingdom of heaven" (Matt. 5:10). While some Christians undergoing trials resort to pity parties, James invites his readers to see the happiness in trials and look beyond them to the glorious end—the kingdom of heaven—and make that the motivation for continued endurance.

The Wise and the Wavering

James 1:4 ends with the notion that those who allow trials to have their way will be perfect and complete, lacking nothing. Verse 5 looks at the reverse side of that notion and says, "If any of you lacks wisdom, let him ask of God, who gives to all liberally and without reproach, and it will be given to him." Those who have the right attitude toward trials and who take them with joy have wisdom. But those who have the wrong attitude and who let trials master them are unwise. They have not yet attained Christian maturity. Some Christians mentally know how to face difficult circumstances but don't have the experiential understanding. Yet how is wisdom different from knowledge? Put simply, wisdom is the ability to employ knowledge wisely. So if we lack the ability to use knowledge rightly when approaching trials, we must ask God, who gives wisdom liberally to those who ask. What the verse suggests is that Christians need wisdom and faith to cope with trials and temptations. It encourages us to pray with faith for such wisdom.

The text gives some information about God that the wise will know. First, He is the source of all wisdom. Second, He is powerful enough to supply everyone's needs but chooses to respond only to those who ask. Third, the passage says that God gives generously/liberally. Fourth, it assures Christians that He does not belittle those who ask. Fifth, it promises that He will indeed respond to our requests. The Bible lists several people for whom God came through. It gives examples of others whose petitions God heard and for whom He fulfilled His promises by responding to their prayers.

Verse 6 looks at the wise and the wavering and the difference between them. The wise know how and when to trust God. They trust Him when they need direction and especially for wisdom to endure during trials and adversity. Some give up at those times that they must trust the most. The wise know that when the trusting gets most difficult is when the leaning and believing on God ought to be most passionate. But they know even more. They know to ask God in faith for what they need and then not to do so doubtingly. Faith here means reliance upon, trust in, and confidence in God. In essence faith involves completely turning the life over to God in total dependence. We do not refer to a negative codependent relationship but rather one in which the Christian realizes that success lies in total surrender to God not only as Savior but Lord. Ellen White gives the best description of such faith.

She tells of the Christian band making its way along a narrow path to the kingdom and happening upon a wide chasm. It had no bridge spanning its banks, and it was too wide and deep for the travelers to jump. As they stood wondering how to get across, they saw cords hanging from the skies. Their dilemma lay in the decision as to whether or not to rely on the cords, since they did not know to what they were attached. Some turned back, unwilling to trust a rope enough to swing across the gulf. Others held on to the cord. In their hands it grew large so that they could use it to carry themselves to the safety of the other side.[12] That's the kind of faith Christians need to withstand trying times and difficult circumstances! So the way to trust God is with solid, reliant, and unwavering faith.

Verse 6 treats how not to trust God. It deals with doubt. James says the person who doubts is like a wave of the sea driven and tossed to and fro by the wind. The wavering person has no stability. Please note that for James doubt is not intellectual instability, the first thing that pops in our modern heads. Here he has in mind spiritual wavering or religious instability. James is saying that wavering persons are unsure, fickle, unbalanced, uncertain, and restless. They make a request of God but do not really believe that they will get a positive response, so they shift between hoping and doubting. Such is not a stable faith.

As a conference youth director I would take campers down to the beautiful shores of western Jamaica, where we would watch the waves. We would see a piece of driftwood being shoved about by the waves. It made no progress either in going out to the sea or in making it to the shore. Instead, it went around in circles. I used it to teach the lesson that without a goal or aim in life one just drifts along with the tide like the driftwood. It is also relevant in this context, in which it implies that the doubting Christian just circles around without making any spiritual progress. Such a person is at the mercy of every fierce storm.

Verse 7 tells how such wavering persons should not assume that they will receive anything from the Lord. What does it mean? That they cannot expect to receive answers, since their requests are insincere and lack confidence in God. The issue is not with Him but with them, because their hearts aren't in their petition. Scripture says, "He who comes to God must believe that He is, and that He is a rewarder of those who diligently seek Him" (Heb. 11:6).

Having such a wavering attitude, they have actually predetermined the divine response. They do not really believe God, so how can they expect Him to answer positively? James says that when we petition from such a halfhearted perspective we should not presume that God will hear or answer in the affirmative. Rather, such requesters are in fact double-minded and unstable persons who want to have it both ways, forgetting that Jesus says we must choose whom we will serve, for we cannot obey two masters. What is the difference between a person of faith and a wavering one?

According to James, the wise person seeks God for wisdom and makes requests in faith without entertaining doubt. The wise have a faith that nothing can destroy. It can withstand the pressures and testing from any foe and will not falter on the edge of or in the midst of poverty or woe. The unwise lack such faith as well as the requisite wisdom. They crumble under the slightest pressure. We find here two divergent approaches to life. The true believer cannot have both. No God-fearers[13] are allowed—for we cannot sit on the fence. It must be one or the other. Which will it be for you?

The Reversal Motif

James opens the next section with a motif strong in the book of Luke generally and Mary's Magnificat particularly. I call it the reversal motif. It sets the tone of the book and is a significant theme. Because he wrote as early as he did, we cannot dismiss it just as acquaintance with Luke's Gospel or with Luke himself. One must therefore conclude that it is familiarity with the source, Mary. God's blessings in the book of Luke come to the poor, the outcast, the marginalized, and women—not to the rich. In the Magnificat, Mary praises God for bypassing the rich and famous and rewarding her who was of lowly estate by making her the mother of the Messiah. If Luke could have heard this to write about it, James must have known it himself and been influenced by it.

James 1:9, 10 says: "Let the lowly brother glory in his exaltation, but the rich in his humiliation." Here is a complete reversal of modern practice and prevailing expectations. What exaltation does a lowly Christian have and what humiliation is there for the rich? By using "but" and "brother," it appears James is taking us back to verse 2, in which he invited the Christian to feel joy in trials and temptations. He is thereby suggesting that the lowly Christians can count themselves as exalted because of their having adopted the right attitude toward suffering and the trust and reliance on God required for it. It means that while lowly Christians may not have many material possessions, they may be spiritually rich and can be happy and joyous knowing they will have peace and security in God. Such persons are in a better place than their counterparts who have everything the world affords but are poor spiritually. Thus lowly Christians must look beyond present circumstances and take pride in their exalted position in Christ.

The Christian ought not to be jealous of the rich, for their realities are different. I am reminded of the proverb that says we should not criticize our neighbor until we have walked a mile in their moccasins. Similarly, Christians ought not to be envious of the rich unless they have trod in their footsteps. James then begins to share a little of the reality of the rich. He says the wealthy person is like a plant that will soon pass away. As soon as the sun rises with a burning heat, it withers the grass. Its beautiful appearance perishes. James's imagery is rich and poignant. We admire the beauty of flowers, especially roses. Yet such beauty does not last. We can admire them for a few days but if we touch them, they lose their attractiveness because they are fleeting. And even if we don't handle them, their beauty will soon be gone, for flowers are temporary gifts from God that momentarily brighten our environment. That is why it is necessary to have the right attitude and why a lowly individual with Christ is richer than a wealthy person without Him.

James says it is similar with wealth. It is just as inviting and eye-catching but it is equally transient. Yet even if it serves its owner for a lifetime, it cannot last forever. The rich also will fade away and cannot take wealth with them. Longenecker is correct: "One danger of wealth is the illusion of permanence that it gives."[14] Wealth and the social status going with it don't last. So the true Christian must not envy or become disillusioned by the apparent success and happiness of the rich person. Christians must seek a better anchor—one rooted in Christ and having the status and security that come with it. That is a far greater joy and a much better happiness. It is one that will outlast time and bear fruit eternally. But the converse is also true. It means that the rich person, if they are to be deemed wise, must have a better anchor. They need to experience the exalted state achievable in God and the joy in Christ. Part of the Christian's duty and obligation to fellow humans is to introduce them to it.

We must explore one final point. Since the relationship between rich and poor is the first thing James mentions here after James 1:8, does this say it is one of the trials that the members of his congregation faced, as some commentators suggest? Were the rich vaunting their wealth and treating the lowly in an unbecoming manner? That is possible, and we will examine more about this in succeeding chapters. Nevertheless, what is important here is that James has done a complete reversal of roles in this section. What we might expect said of the rich we instead hear of the lowly, and the converse is also true—the unexpected was reported of the rich.

It is possible that after the first resurrection, some we expect to be there will not be, while others we thought would be excluded will in fact be present. How good that we don't make the determination but that God and only He will. In which group will you find yourself? You are making that decision now in your choices. Let's be sure to make the correct ones. But never forget that on the glorious reunion morning Jesus is going to say to the Father, "These are they which came out of great tribulation, and have washed their robes, and made them white in the blood of the Lamb" (Rev. 7:14, KJV).

Application

Does this message apply to us today? If we are indeed near the end, then the time of great tribulation looms upon us. And if it is, we will need endurance. James's counsel to regard trials joyously is therefore relevant. Many Christians who are becoming discouraged, listless, indifferent, and cold as a result of the trials they face need such a message.

They also must hear James's teaching that tribulation has a role in eternal preparation—it produces authentic disciples. Disciples who endure temptations and trials are not only happy during the process, counting it joy, and happy at the end at having endured, but James says that they will be rewarded. The English versions promise "the crown of life" (James 1:12), but a better rendering of the Greek would be "the crown which is life" or "the crown consisting of life." Just as our Master endured and was highly exalted at His return to glory, even so authentic disciples will share in the heavenly blessings and life everlasting—the ultimate reward. Count it a joy to endure trials and tribulation and get ready for the great getting-up morning.

---

[1] A. T. Robertson, *Word Pictures,* vol. 6, p. 11.

[2] *The SDA Bible Commentary,* vol. 7, p. 503.

[3] Robertson, vol. 6, p. 11.

[4] I-Jin Loh and Howard A. Hatton, *A Translator's Handbook on the Letter From James,* online ed. (New York: United Bible Societies, 1997), pp. 11, 12.

[5] Robertson, vol. 6, p. 11.

[6] *Ibid.*

[7] *Ibid.*

[8] Loh and Hatton, pp. 11, 12.

[9] Joseph B. Mayor, *The Epistle of St. James,* online ed. (n.p., n.d.), p. 32.

[10] *The SDA Bible Commentary,* vol. 7, p. 504.

[11] Robertson, vol. 6, p. 12.

[12] Ellen G. White, *Testimonies for the Church* (Mountain View, Calif.: Pacific Press Pub. Assn., 1948), vol. 2, pp. 594-597.

[13] God-fearers were Gentiles who tacitly accepted Judaism of the first century. They would attend and make gifts to the synagogue but would not go the full way of taking on the whole yoke of the Torah and proselyte baptism. Christianity, especially through Paul, gained a lot of converts from their ranks.

[14] Richard Longenecker, ed., *Patterns of Discipleship in the New Testament* (Grand Rapids: Wm. B. Eerdmans, 1996), p. 233.

CHAPTER 3

The Key to Rooting Out Desire

We now return to the issue of temptations and trials and will seek their source. Horace Walpole used to say, "Every man has his price."[1] Would James agree? It is an interesting question, especially since he took time in this section to make sure that his readers understood the function of desire in sin and the key to rooting it out.

To give context to our study, we'll examine the views of some contemporaries of James and that of at least three world religions. Contemporary Greeks of James's day had a perspective on the issue. For them, the prevailing notion was that the gods were responsible for the temptations of humans and thus carried the blame for the resultant sin.[2]

Barclay sees in Judaism a tendency on the part of some to blame God for evil. Using the author of Ecclesiasticus as an example, he showed how Jewish thought on the origin of evil traced it back to Satan. God created humans and left them as prey in the hands of the foe. Other Jewish writers also pushed the evil tendency in humans back to the Garden of Eden. Taking the form of an angel and speaking through the serpent, Satan instilled in Eve a desire for the forbidden with which, at the serpent's bidding, she lured Adam. Some believe that Satan placed the poison of his malice (lust and desire) in the fruit—lust being the beginning of all sin. Some even came to see that the beginning of all sin was Satan's lust for Eve.[3]

Several other theories emerged among the Jews, but, in the opinion of Barclay, they all shoved the problem further back. But the issue of ultimate origin had to be solved. Some of the rabbis in seeking to unravel the mystery made God responsible, for if He created everything, He must have originated evil.[4] In sum, what is significant here is sin has its origin in desire and thus God is ultimately responsible for evil.

Still another world religion also saw desire, good or bad, as being the culprit. Its founder spent long days and hours seeking enlightenment and could not attain it. When he stopped desiring it, it came. For this religion, to live is to suffer, and the reason for suffering is that we have desire that can only lead to disappointment. If we can somehow root out desire and eliminate its hold on us, then we could cause suffering to stop. That particular religion decided that the best way to stop desire was following the path outlined by its founder—right views, right intention, right speech, right effort, right action, right livelihood, right mindfulness, and right concentration. Again, desire lurks at the core of the problem, but it is human effort through an eightfold path that will bring change. While it contributes to understanding desire's role in sin, such human effort can't resolve the dilemma of sin. So let's see James's views on the subject.

The Source of Temptation

First, on the issue of the source of temptation, James says that no one should "say when . . . tempted, 'I am tempted by God'" (James 1:13). He raises an agelong dilemma. Is God responsible for temptation or not? On the surface it seems like a trivial question, but it is by no means so. If God does not send temptation, how do we explain 1 Corinthians 10:13: "No temptation has overtaken you except such as is common to man; but God *is* faithful, who will not allow you to be tempted beyond what you are able, but with the temptation will also make the way of escape, that you may be able to bear it." Or, again, how does James match this statement with that in James 1:2, in which he states that we should count it joy when we fall into various temptations? To begin with, we need to note a few things.

The first text (1 Cor. 10:13) does not claim that God is responsible for temptation. Rather, it speaks to God's faithfulness and dependability. We can trust His being with us in the crucible of trials as He was with the Hebrew young men in the fiery furnace. 2. It simply says that God will not allow us to endure more temptation than we can bear. That's something to recall when facing trials. God determines its severity. He has confidence in us that we can withstand whatever comes our way, but that does not attribute the responsibility to Him. 3. The passage has a promise in it. God states He will make a way of escape from all temptation. We don't have to succumb. There will be a way out. 4. We will be able to bear it. God will be beside us in those difficult moments to assist us. But we definitely find no blame here placed on Him for temptation.

The second text (James 1:2), as we have seen, describes how we should relate toward trial and temptation. While it urges us to count it joy, it doesn't say that God sends the temptation. Here we have counsel to adopt the right attitude to temptation, not blame God for it. James's position is correct. To claim that God tempts us is to fall victim to the blame game. And what is that? It's the human tendency to shift rather than accept responsibility. After the first sin, Adam and Eve went in hiding when they heard God coming. When called out, Adam said he heard God in the garden and was afraid because he was naked and thus hid. Note Adam's response when asked how he knew he was naked: "The woman whom You gave to be with me, she gave me of the tree, and I ate" (Gen. 3:12). He took no responsibility for his actions.

Then when God asks the woman what she had done, she tells Him, "The serpent deceived me, and I ate" (verse 13). If they are our foreparents, is it any marvel that after sin has ravaged the world for thousands of years some of us still accept no responsibility for our actions but blame everyone else? Yet since God created everything and since He said that everything was very good, was He responsible for originating evil? To put it another way, since God made Lucifer, who became the devil and who deceived Eve, should we hold Him accountable for sin? Be careful how you answer such questions, lest you join the blame game too!

With James we can conclude that God didn't originate evil and does not tempt us with it. Who then is responsible for suffering? The Bible attributes culpability to the devil and his imps. Paul says, "For we wrestle not against flesh and blood, but against principalities, against powers, against the rulers of the darkness of this world, against spiritual wickedness in high places" (Eph. 6:12, KJV). They do bad things to people and influence them to blame a good God. So don't be fooled.

The story of the Gadarene demoniacs is a classic example of how they work. Rejected by society, forsaken by friends, spurned by family, and possessed by demons, the men lived among the tombs—a religiously taboo place for Jews. They were so violent that no one could pass that way. When Jesus arrived on the scene, the demons asked if He had come to torment them prematurely. Even they know Jesus and His power. Yet some humans trifle with Him. Recognizing their vulnerability before Him, the demons begged to enter a herd of pigs feeding nearby. But when given permission, they made the animals jump off a cliff into the water. Nevertheless, when the herders reported the loss to the townspeople, the devil inveigled them to blame Jesus for it. The sight of men who had once been a threat to themselves and society now restored to their right minds meant nothing to the Gadarenes. The devil had skewed them to love things and use people. He delights in doing bad things and influencing people to blame a good God for them.

In Eden he used the serpent as a medium through which to deceive the woman. In the wilderness he went to Jesus pretending to be an angel of light from heaven in answer to His prayer.[5] He still walks around like a roaring lion seeking whom he may devour (1 Peter 5:8). While the devil tempts, we yield and obey. The usual alibi does not work. The devil can't make anyone do anything that they don't want to do. We can't evade our complicity in wrong and culpability for sin. James declares that while the devil tempts, we respond out of our own desire (James 1:14).

Desire's Role in Temptation

Second, let's explore the issue of desire and its relation to temptation and trials. The apostle James clearly states that God does not tempt anyone. From where, then, do temptations come? "Each one is tempted when he is drawn away by his own desires and enticed" (verse 14), the apostle explains. We are lured away by our own desires. The word "enticed" has a fishing background. It refers to catching fish with bait.[6] James, a Christian author, joins other world religions in attributing temptations to desire. Are they correct? Let's use the experience of the two Adams as test cases.

Genesis 3 tells us that humans took three downward steps that led them astray: Eve listened to wrong (verses 1-3), doubted God (verses 4, 5), and then believed a lie (verse 6). She accepted the tempter's word above her Creator's. How could she do that and why did she do so? Verse 6 explains that she saw that the tree was good for food, pleasing to the eyes, and something to be desired to make her wise. Her decision to eat resulted from feelings stirred by the serpent's words. Influenced by what pleased the eyes and supposedly could make one wise, those desires led to an even greater one—the desire to be like God, as promised by the enemy (verse 5). Eve's experience not only supports the idea that desire inspires sin but also shows that the enemy does not always deliver what he offers, and by the time a person discovers that fact, it is too late. But what of Adam's experience?

Can you appreciate his dilemma on discovering Eve's choice? He had observed his uniqueness among the animals—the only species without a complementary partner. It had created loneliness and then desire for a companion. God satisfied that longing when He created a being for him whom Adam named "woman," since God had taken her from man. Excited, he had said that at last here was someone of his own bone and flesh. Now she had disobeyed God and was inviting him to join her in wrong. Ellen White says sadness crossed his face at the temptation and he had a terrible struggle in his mind.[7] Adam "had looked upon the glory of the Creator. He understood the high destiny opened to the human race should they remain faithful to God. Yet all these blessings were lost sight of in the fear of losing that one gift which in his eyes outvalued every other. . . . He resolved to share her fate; if she must die, he would die with her."[8] Here is an example of plain desire—desire to have and be with his wife. We can also view it from another perspective—desire not to lose his wife.

James is right. Desire lies at the root of most, if not all, temptations. What makes it so powerful and what gives it such a grip on us? Rooted in humans is a certain degree of curiosity upon which the enemy thrives. Paul says, "But sin, taking opportunity by the commandment, produced in me all manner of evil desire" (Rom. 7:8). One would have thought the entrance of law, which gives knowledge of sin, would have curbed sin. Instead, it caused sin to multiply. The craving for the unknown fuels it.

A story tells of a man who always blamed Adam and Eve for sin. Growing tired of hearing his complaints, a friend invited him to housesit while he went on vacation. He left everything in the house at his disposal except a small box sitting in a corner. That was off-limits, the friend said, and he shouldn't open it. The first man agreed to the terms. Unfortunately, he couldn't contain his curiosity or control his desire to see what the box contained. Within a half hour of his friend's departure he had opened the box. When he did, a rat jumped out and disappeared. The man spent the rest of the time in turmoil; he tried to locate the rat or get another one for the box, but couldn't. When his friend returned and saw what curiosity and desire had done, he admonished him to stop blaming Adam and Eve for sin, since he was just as guilty. That's how desire works.

James makes an interesting point in James 1:15: "When desire has conceived, it gives birth to sin." Are James and Paul at odds on the issue? After all, Paul says in Romans 7:8 (as we saw) that sin using the law produced all kinds of evil desires. Now James says desire, when conceived, gives birth to sin. A closer look will reveal that the seeming conflict is only apparent, not real. What Paul has in mind is that we would assume that knowledge of wrong as derived from law should have curbed sin, for a realization of what is wrong should lead to a decision to avoid it. Yet, he argues, knowledge instead aroused curiosity and created desire for the unknown. If sin is the "transgression of the law" (1 John 3:4, KJV), and if knowledge of wrong stimulates cravings for it, then the end result of yielding to those cravings would be more sin. That is precisely what Paul means.

Looking at salvation from a historical perspective, he is saying that between Adam and Moses, people were alive without a written codification of the law, but when God spoke and codified the commandment at Sinai, sin multiplied instead of being curbed. In sum, Paul's point is that the law created curiosity and desire, causing sin to mushroom. Sin exploited the law to produce further desire and curiosity that led to still more sin, resulting in death.

And that is precisely what James articulates. Desire—another designation for lust—fuels the temptation train. However we might refer to it, it is a tool of sin. Christians need to understand and be aware of how it operates. Ellen White tells us that "the tenth commandment strikes at the very root of all sins, prohibiting the selfish desire, from which springs the sinful act."[9] Finally, when desire has had its full term, it gives birth to sin; and when sin is fully grown, it issues in death. So both James and Paul agree that death is the ripened product of sin, and desire is its mastermind, agent, and propagator.

Judaism, Buddhism, and Christianity conclude that desire lies at the root of evil and if left uncurbed will lead to ruin. The key question now concerns how to eliminate such a destructive monster. And that is where the various religions part company. Judaism's emphasis on law and doing is legendary. Its expression in Jesus' time viewed sin as a wrong act and righteousness as a good deed to right that wrong. So if a person's good deeds balanced or outweighed the bad deeds, then the person was righteous. Thus while the law required fasting annually,[10] Jews fasted twice a week to accumulate merits. They also believed that Abraham had amassed enough merits to cover them. Furthermore, they assumed that when the Messiah arrived He would transform the present evil age into the age to come, one that would herald everlasting blessedness. Thus we can see why Paul's conversion to Christianity was so radical—why he so vehemently opposed works righteousness and why his contemporaries determined to destroy him.

For Buddhism, rooting out desire is the key issue. Gautama did not attain enlightenment when he desired and sought it. But when he abandoned desire, enlightenment came. Life is an endless cycle of recurring desires and cravings. To eliminate desire, one must do the right thing, which is following the path he outlined—right views, right intention, right speech, right effort, right action, right livelihood, right mindfulness, and right concentration. While they may be good in and of themselves, they are still human-based, and alone or even collectively, they cannot get rid of either desire or the sin problem. What sets Christianity apart from the other world religions is that not only does it have a good answer for the origin of evil—it has the solution.

On reading Philippians 2:12 ("Therefore, my beloved, as you have always obeyed, not as in my presence only, but now much more in my absence, work out your own salvation with fear and trembling"), some Christians assume that we must produce our own salvation. But when salvation is concerned, human effort is not only fruitless but futile. Paul correctly says that deeds of the law shall never justify us in God's sight (Rom. 3:20). It not only outlaws human activity as a means of salvation, but brings God into the picture. Human effort is unable to deliver us from desire or sin's power. We need a power outside of and beyond ourselves for that. And that's why God sent a Creator to be Redeemer. Paul puts it beautifully: "God was in Christ, reconciling the world unto himself" (2 Cor. 5:19, KJV).

Jesus is God's answer to the problem of evil. Back in the Garden of Eden the Lord had told Adam and Eve that the day they ate of the tree of the knowledge of good and of evil they would surely die. They ate, but though they died spiritually and morally that day, physical death was not instantaneous. God had put in "layaway" a special plan to meet such an exigency. That is why Scripture refers to Jesus as the lamb slain from before the foundation of the world. On the day of the very first sin, God made a promise that we have come to know as the everlasting covenant. God declared: "I will put enmity between thee and the woman, and between thy seed and her seed; it shall bruise thy head, and thou shalt bruise his heel" (Gen. 3:15, KJV). He fulfilled that promise through Jesus of Nazareth. That is why the angel told Joseph, "Thou son of David, fear not to take unto thee Mary thy wife: for that which is conceived in her is of the Holy Ghost. And she shall bring forth a son, and thou shalt call his name Jesus: for he shall save his people from their sins" (Matt. 1:20, 21, KJV). Furthermore, it is why John said, "For God so loved the world, that he gave his only begotten Son, that whosoever believeth in him should not perish, but have everlasting life" (John 3:16, KJV). And it is the way the early church interpreted the death of Jesus, as we can see from Hebrews 10:5-10:

"Therefore, when He came into the world, He said:
'Sacrifice and offering You did not desire,
But a body You have prepared for Me.
In burnt offerings and sacrifices for sin
You had no pleasure.
Then I said, "Behold, I have come—
In the volume of the book it is written of Me—
To do Your will, O God."'

"Previously saying, 'Sacrifice and offering, burnt offerings, and offerings for sin You did not desire, nor had pleasure in them' (which are offered according to the law), then He said, 'Behold, I have come to do Your will, O God.' He takes away the first that He may establish the second. By that will we have been sanctified through the offering of the body of Jesus Christ once for all."

Obviously, here is God's answer to the problem of evil. Yet how does the individual believer appropriate it? John 3:16 says the gift is for those who believe. It requires faith on the part of the individual believer. However, belief and faith are not the same thing. The devils believe and even tremble but will not be saved, since they do not have the requisite faith. It requires saving faith—belief put in action by acceptance of the gift. God has made the necessary provision, but we must individually accept it. That is why Paul says in Ephesians 2:8, 9: "For by grace you have been saved [*God's part*] through faith [*our part/response*], and that not of yourselves; it is the gift of God, not of works, lest anyone should boast." We must respond by accepting it, but our acceptance is not a work. Neither can we work to purchase or procure it. It is a free gift of God. Nor will any of us go to heaven and, when we can't have it our way, challenge God by asserting that we can do anything we want because we purchased salvation or worked our way to it. That shall never happen. We must accept God's terms, or we will not receive His salvation. Self must be put aside for God's way. While in ordinary life we might not cherish things that are free, this is one free gift that must be prized. Also, we must not fail to note that while salvation is free, it is not cheap—it cost God His only begotten Son and required the life of Jesus. Christ paid the full price of our salvation—all of it. That is why I love Him and have accepted His offer of salvation.

But how do we work out our salvation? What was Paul talking about? If we look at the context, we will find that what goes before this passage is the exaltation of Christ after He humbled Himself to redeem us. By reason of what He did and His subsequent exaltation, every knee shall bow before Him and every tongue confess His lordship to the glory of the Father. Thus the context of the passage calls for consistency in profession of faith and practice, not just in the presence of Paul their teacher and founder but also in his absence. Church members are to stand for what they know and believe to be right. The word used for "work" implies continuing on to the finish.[11] Referencing individual freedom and responsibility in the matter of their salvation, it is an exhortation for Christians to carry out their salvation "to completion."[12] Philippians 2:13, in which Paul says, "It is God who works in you both to will and to do for His good pleasure," supports the fact that it is what God calls us to do and not a demand for salvation by works.

Thus we work out our salvation not by deeds performed but by deliberate exercise of the will. We do so by choosing to remain in the sphere of Christ's influence. Ellen White concurs: "You are not able, of yourself, to bring your purposes and desires and inclinations into submission to the will of God; but if you are 'willing to be made willing,' God will accomplish the work for you, even 'casting down imaginations, and every high thing that exalteth itself against the knowledge of God, and bringing into captivity every thought to the obedience of Christ,' 2 Corinthians 10:5. Then you will 'work out your own salvation with fear and trembling.'"[13]

How do we do this? I find four aspects of Christian life especially helpful—prayer, Bible study, Christian witnessing, and living as though we were always in Jesus' own presence. The latter requires us to live as though we are standing before Christ Himself, for in fact we always are but don't always recognize that fact. This then is a call to regulate our lives accordingly. When we pray constantly, feed on the Word incessantly, share our faith—the best way to keep our faith is to give it away—and live each moment as with God Himself, we can describe it as walking with God. When Moses had such an association with God on the mount for 40 days, his face shone with divine glory. And when we get to that place with God and reflect His glory in our lives and faces, it takes care of evil desires and sin without our even trying. What a tremendous benefit for a wonderful practice and an awesome relationship!

Required Qualities for Facing Trials

In James 1:16 the apostle admonishes his readers to avoid deception. Put positively, it is a call to honesty and truthfulness. To ensure a positive outcome, he further endears himself to them by designating them "my beloved brethren." He seeks to prevent them from letting Satan lead them astray. Perhaps he intended his admonition to build on a verb in verse 14 that implied catching a fish by bait or being enticed by pleasure. Together they would appeal for believers to avoid being deceived into thinking that God is responsible for sin or being enticed by the pleasures of desire and sin into losing their way.

This leads to verse 17, in which he gives the source of all good gifts. Apparently James now returns to a line of argument he began in verse 13. His trend of thought suggests that any desire leading to enticements that manifest themselves in sin that then bear fruit in death clearly can't be good. Thus, how could we blame God for them? I hear the apostle exclaiming, "God forbid!" So to make it absolutely clear that the Lord is not to be associated with evil, he repeats himself, but this time he puts it in the positive: "Every good gift and every perfect gift is from above, and comes down from the Father of lights, with whom there is no variation or shadow of turning" (verse 17). If every good and perfect gift is from above, and God doesn't give harmful gifts to His children, imperfect gifts don't come from Him but must have their source elsewhere—with the father of lies, the deceiver, the devil.

The fact that James says good and perfect gifts originate from our heavenly Father suggests he has more in mind. While all gifts have their origin in God, only one gift was good and perfect and came down from above: "For God so loved the world that He gave His only begotten Son, that whoever believes in Him should not perish but have everlasting life" (John 3:16). That this is James's intent James 1:18 clearly brings out. James says that of His own will and by His own word of truth God brought us forth to become firstfruits of His creatures. Jesus Christ, whom God gave as a ransom for sin, came from the Father of lights as the "true Light" from which all human beings must be lit. This could therefore be a reference to salvation. God is the source of all genuine gifts, and so gifts that are not good cannot originate in or with Him, for He is not fickle—He is the paragon of virtue and consistency and far exceeds anyone or anything else. Thus Christians need belief in and dependence upon the God of virtue and consistency as they face the temptations of a wily foe.

In verse 19 James exhorts his readers once more, employing the endearing "my beloved brethren." Now the invitation is to be "swift to hear, slow to speak, and slow to wrath." It is excellent advice for every Christian but especially leaders. Too many of us love to hear our own voices so much that even when we pretend to be listening to others what we are really doing is thinking about what we are going to say next. Thus we disrespect others by either interrupting them or making inappropriate responses.

Fascinatingly, when James mentions "slow to speak," he's referring not to hesitation in speaking but rather to caution in starting to speak. He encourages his readers to think before they open their mouths. A good rule of thumb is to pause a moment before we respond to someone else. This will allow us time to digest and reflect on what another has said. Too many of us speak and then think rather than the reverse. James's readers seem to have had this age-old problem. Let's note the following examples that show the widespread nature of the problem.

"In the Sayings of the Jewish Fathers we read: 'There are four characters in scholars. Quick to hear and quick to forget; his gain is cancelled by his loss. Slow to hear and slow to forget; his loss is cancelled by his gain. Quick to hear and slow to forget; he is wise. Slow to hear and quick to forget; this is an evil lot.' Ovid bids men to be slow to punish, but swift to reward. Philo bids a man to be swift to benefit others, and slow to harm them. . . . Hort says that the really good man will be much more anxious to listen to God than arrogantly, garrulously and stridently to shout his own opinions. The classical writers had the same idea. Zeno said, 'We have two ears but only one mouth, that we may hear more and speak less.' When Demonax was asked how a man might rule best, he answered, 'Without anger, speaking little, and listening much.' Bias said, 'If you hate quick speaking, you will not fall into error.' The tribute was once paid to a great linguist that he could be silent in seven different languages."[14]

It is still a problem for contemporary Christians. Thus we find much here from which we can and should benefit. We need to learn from nature. God showed the way by endowing us with one mouth and two ears. While for Zeno it meant that we must hear more and speak less, for me it implies that we must listen twice as much as we speak. A friend of mine who has a program emphasizing listening suggests that we need to follow the 80/20 rule—i.e., we must listen 80 percent of the time and speak 20 percent. All of us need to spend more time listening. Also, we should be aware of the difference between listening and hearing. While we may listen and not hear, we can't hear without listening. Because communication is a two-way process, we must not only be willing to speak but also be willing, as recipients, to listen carefully to what another is saying. It is important to note also the different types of listening. Here are nine kinds:

1. Discriminative—the most basic kind is the ability to hear the subtleties of emotional variation in another person's voice.
2. Comprehensive—also called content listening or informative listening, it involves having the vocabulary and tools to understand fully what is being said.
3. Critical or evaluative—listening to evaluate and judge; forming opinions about what is being said; assessing strengths and weaknesses of ideas; giving agreement or approval to the argument.
4. Appreciative—a very enjoyable if not the most pleasurable kind of listening used to assess needs and goals as well as enjoying good music or poetry.
5. Sympathetic—shows care and concern about the other person by paying close attention and expressing sorrow for ills or happiness at joys.
6. Empathetic—goes beyond sympathy to enter into and share the feelings of the speaker.
7. Therapeutic—involves listening that utilizes the deep connections of empathy to understand, change, and develop the speaker.
8. Dialogic—learning what the other person thinks through conversation and an engaged interchange of ideas and information.
9. Relationship—listening to develop and sustain a relationship.[15]

Yet we must remember that not all listening is good or all quickness of speaking bad. Also, we can listen to confirm preconceived notions, find fault in what was said, or to detect error. Some will listen from only a critical or biased perspective. We should avoid such approaches. On the other hand, permissible quick speech includes offering words of cheer, comfort, and peace about divine love and providence, as well as affirming others. As we become less impulsive and impetuous in our speech we will avoid injuring those whom we talk to.

James adds still another dimension to his counsels. He says we should be slow to anger. To me, if we would listen twice as much as we speak, then we would understand more than normal, thus reducing tensions and misapprehensions. As a result, there surely would be less to get angry about. I contend that we can never get upset with someone unless we have compared ourselves with that person and conclude that they are in some manner ahead of us. It can lead to intolerance toward the views and ideas of that person and foster a desire to prove ourselves superior. Such a reaction manifests itself in our wanting to speak more than that person. Envy, jealously, pride—and every other sin, for that matter—stem from the selfsame root. It behooves us then to heed the counsel of the apostle James because it would not only improve our interpersonal relationships but make us better persons. Furthermore, it also implies, I believe, that slowness in speaking will also reduce anger, tension, strife, misunderstanding, and the like. Heeding James's counsel will make us feel not only better about ourselves but good about others. Perhaps Paul's counsel to let love lubricate all our actions and interactions (1 Cor. 16:14) will prove germane here.

But there is still another valid way to view this text. Since James refers to "the word of truth" (James 1:18), and since in those days people heard it corporately and did not read it individually, then a call to be swift to hear could refer to the heard word of truth. Here the intent is for listeners to pay careful attention to the spoken word and then put it into practice. James wants to make sure there is good consistency between word and deed, profession and practice. Robertson comments: "The picture points to listening to the word of truth and is aimed against violent and disputatious speech."[16] In this context slowness of speech would refer to anything that could disrupt the effectiveness of the Word, whether in the congregation where someone is reading it out loud or in the individual's life. There needs to be a consistent witness. Also, slowness of speaking envisions thinking before speaking, which would eliminate problems caused by rash speaking.

We find the rational for the counsel in verse 19 located in verse 20. James says human wrath or anger does not produce the righteousness of God. The reference here is to personal anger. When we speak before we think, leading to reckless comments, we do not represent the Father. The resultant angry, vengeful, envious, jealous, and bitter words wound others unnecessarily and can alienate them from God and right. Such speech would not emphasize the mercy, grace, forgiveness, and love of the Father that Christians have received and ought to reciprocate at all times. That is why James is correct and it is imperative for us to be slow to speak and quick to hear. Hearing things from the other person's perspective can help to calm situations.

Implicit in verse 20 is the notion that the Christian's duty is to accomplish the righteousness of God. We typically define righteousness as rightdoing, but there exists still another way of seeing it. It is an attribute of God—His way of setting humans right with Him. Seen from that perspective, James says boiling rage or vengeful speech do not set people right with God, which is what salvation is all about. To accomplish that we need peace, healing, mercy, justice, truth, fellowship, and love. All our actions and interactions as Christians should seek those ends.

Application

To conclude this section, James says, "Therefore lay aside all filthiness and overflow of wickedness, and receive with meekness the implanted word, which is able to save your souls" (verse 21). We could render the "therefore" as "on this basis." On what basis? That of doing what pleases God and accomplishes His purpose. What should Christians do? They should put off anything that defiles as they would dirty clothing. Barclay says the word used in Greek is derived from one that when employed medically connotes wax in the ear.[17] In essence James invites his readers to remove anything and everything that would clog their ears to God's true Word.

He urges them to avoid malice, envy, strife, or anything separating them from neighbor or God. Nothing must interfere with or hinder free access between the soul and God. Christians should receive with humility the implanted Word—the gospel truth—that is able to effect salvation since it connects us with the Master. So, speak less; listen more; promote that which leads to salvation; avoid anything that defiles; and receive the Word of truth that has the potential of effecting salvation. Excellent advice for successful discipleship at any time, it especially applies now in the twenty-first century.

---

[1] Quoted in Gordon Nasby, ed., *Treasury of the Christian World* (New York: Harper and Brothers, 1953), p. 352.

[2] *The SDA Bible Commentary*, vol. 7, p. 509.

[3] W. Barclay, *The Letters to the Corinthians*, pp. 45-51.

[4] *Ibid.* Cf. Peter H. Davids, *The Epistle of James: A Commentary on the Greek Text*, online ed. (Grand Rapids: Wm. B. Eerdmans, 1982).

[5] Ellen G. White, *The Desire of Ages*, p. 118.

[6] A. T. Robertson, *Word Pictures*, vol. 6, p. 18.

[7] Ellen G. White, *Patriarchs and Prophets* (Mountain View, Calif.: Pacific Press Pub. Assn., 1956), p. 56.

[8] *Ibid.*

[9] *Ibid.*, p. 309.

[10] See Robertson, vol. 2, p. 233.

[11] Robertson, vol. 4, p. 446.

[12] *The SDA Bible Commentary*, vol. 7, p. 158.

[13] Ellen G. White, *Thoughts From the Mount of Blessing* (Washington, D.C.: Review

and Herald Pub. Assn., 1956), p. 142.

[14] William Barclay, *The Letters of James and Peter,* rev. ed. (Philadelphia: Westminster Press, 1975), p. 55.

[15] See http://changingminds.org/techniques/listening/types_listening.htm.

[16] Robertson, vol. 6, p. 21.

[17] Barclay, *The Letters of James and Peter,* p. 57.

CHAPTER 4

Reversing the Disconnect

Some years ago I researched why youth leave the church. The number one issue they stated was the inconsistency between profession and practice among adults. That's James's concern in James 1:22-27. He begins, "But be doers of the word, and not hearers only, deceiving yourselves. For if anyone is a hearer of the word and not a doer, he is like a man observing his natural face in a mirror; for he observes himself, goes away, and immediately forgets what kind of man he was." How do we resolve the incongruity between walk and talk, faith and profession?

Years ago the dangers of cigarette smoking came to light. The surgeon general even prints a warning label on each pack detailing its harmful effects. Yet the World Health Organization estimates 1.3 billion people worldwide smoke, and every 6.5 seconds a current or former smoker dies. Despite such warnings, approximately 6 million deaths occur yearly as a result of tobacco smoking, and it will kill 8.3 million in 2030.[1] People hear the warning, see the labels, know the harmful effects, yet continue to do what they know damages their bodies. As Christians who don't smoke, we often berate and condemn them—but are we any better? We read and listen to the Word of truth, yet we too find it hard to do what we know is right. Although we hear the Word, we don't act on it.

Thus we confront a disconnect between who we say we are, what we say we do, and how we really perform. Said another way, we here encounter the gap that exists between faith and practice; walk and talk; profession and performance. James shows that it isn't a new phenomenon. It has been an agelong challenge for those who profess religion and seek to translate it into daily life. Let me share an experience to illustrate the point. My mother sold books to secure my education. One summer I decided to assist her. On a street in Montego Bay, Jamaica, called Love Lane, I met a woman who wanted a set of *Bedtime Stories*. She did not have all the money, so she gave a deposit and made an appointment for me to return for the final payment.

On the appointed day I turned up, knocked at the gate, and waited. Instead of the mother, her 12-year-old daughter met me. "Mama says I must tell you she is not here." Since then I have wondered how her mother responded the next time the girl told her a lie. Did she know she was teaching her daughter to do exactly that? Too many parents, teachers, and Christians preach a dogma called "do as I say, not as I do." Yet people learn more from what they see and experience than from what they hear. That's why we must ensure that our walk and our talk cohere. We must remember that what we do affects others more than what we say, and what we do touches the lives of others more profoundly than what they hear us say. Let's keep consistent.

Note James's loving plea to his readers: "But be doers of the word, and not hearers only" (verse 22). Here he agrees with Paul, who said, "For not the hearers of the law are just in the sight of God, but the doers of the law will be justified" (Rom. 2:13). For contemporary readers they might have said, "Not the readers of the Word are just in the sight of God, but the doers of the law are justified." The point here is that those who are blessed and who are justified are those who put into practice what they have read or heard. Too many are satisfied with mere profession with no performance. They are the ones that James targets.

He says that those who hear the Word but don't practice it only delude themselves. Convincing themselves that they have a genuine relationship with God when in fact they do not, they have come to believe their own lies. We can compare them to those who look at self in the mirror and soon forget what they saw. A look in the mirror of Calvary reveals all that Christ did to redeem us from sin and therefore shows what we ought to do in thankful appreciation for His incomprehensible sacrifice. While we cannot repay Him and while He does not require payment, the least we can do is render loving, consistent witness to the merits of His grace and the effectiveness of His transforming power in lives. Although true Christian living isn't a work of law and while there is nothing salvific about it, it is not a Christian option—rather it is a Christian imperative. It is our way of demonstrating the marvelous grace of Him who called us from darkness into His marvelous light (1 Peter 2:9).

Those who hear the Word but don't do it also deceive themselves in still another way. They suppose they have a relationship with God and are heading for the kingdom when in fact they are not. Some forget the words of Jesus: "Not everyone who says to Me, 'Lord, Lord,' shall enter the kingdom of heaven, but he who does the will of My Father in heaven" (Matt. 7:21). While our works cannot save us, a lack of them can exclude us from the kingdom. Jesus infers that doing the heavenly Father's will is a prerequisite for entrance. While works can't earn salvation, as some religionists believe, they are indispensable to the spiritual life. What then is the role of works in salvation? We'll pursue this subject in a later chapter, for it is important to James. But for the moment we can note that deeds are the fruits of salvation—not its means. They don't earn salvation. Instead, they are the natural products of a spiritual life.

How does this work? Doers of the Word recognize they are blessed to bless. It means they know the blessings and privileges of salvation are not theirs to hoard and enjoy. With them comes the obligation to invite others to taste and see that the Lord is good (Ps. 34:8). Abram's experience illustrates the principle. God called him from Ur of the Chaldeans to a land He would show him. As part of the package, God told him:

"I will bless you
And make your name great;
And you shall be a blessing.
I will bless those who bless you,
And I will curse him who curses you;
And in you all the families of the earth shall be blessed" (Gen. 12:2, 3).

We find here both the reciprocal nature of blessings and the blessed-to-bless principle. God told Abraham, "I will bless you, make your name great, bless those who bless you, and curse those who curse you." The divine activity represents the vertical aspect of blessings. Our reaching out to others is the horizontal aspect. The Lord blesses us so that we can bless others. When God told Abraham, "You shall be a blessing," He spoke of the horizontal plane of blessing. God also emphasized it by adding, "And in you all the families of the earth shall be blessed." So as God reached down vertically to bless Abraham, God expected him to reach out horizontally to bless all the families of the earth. After receiving blessings, Abraham blessed Lot and the Canaanite kings with whom he fought. He blessed them with all the spoils, taking none, though he was entitled to them. He blessed as he was blessed.

The prophet Micah also illustrates the vertical and horizontal aspects of the Christian life. To the people's questions about what God required of them, and if their offerings and sacrifices would appease Him, Micah gave an unmistakable answer:

"He has shown you, O man, what is good;
And what does the Lord require of you
But to do justly,
To love mercy,
And to walk humbly with your God?" (Micah 6:8).

That the context is salvation and its requirements we can ascertain from its liberation overtone. God has been the speaker in the earlier verses of the chapter. He brings a complaint against Israel and asks what He has done to weary them. Then He invites them to testify against Him. In its context, God speaks of liberating them from Egyptian bondage and from Balak at the time of Balaam. The Lord even gives a rationale for His deliverance—that they "may know the righteousness of the Lord" (verse 5). It was in their attempts to appease God that Israel asked what they should bring before Him. That this was their intent we see in the superfluous nature of their response:

"With what shall I come before the Lord,
And bow myself before the High God?
Shall I come before Him with burnt offerings,
With calves a year old?
Will the Lord be pleased with thousands of rams,
Ten thousand rivers of oil?
Shall I give my firstborn for my transgression,
The fruit of my body for the sin of my soul?" (verses 6, 7).

In such a context Micah's response is even more remarkable. He says that God has already shown what to do and what He requires. Yet he sums it all up for them in a triad—to do justly, love mercy, and walk humbly with God. To act justly is to demonstrate a passionate regard for right and to treat fellow humans with dignity, fair play, truth, and justice. It requires Christians to defend the outcast, the defenseless, the dispossessed, the marginalized, and the poor and needy ones. To love mercy is to be empathetic, kind, understanding, and reasonable. The first two traits give the horizontal dimension of the Christian relationship, since they involve interpersonal relations. The last item, walking humbly with God, gives the vertical dimension, as it summons Christians to be humble in their relationship and to walk with God who is Creator, Savior, and Friend.

Such a triad calls for Christian life in the marketplace to agree with that in the worshipplace. It summons Christians to live on Main Street as they do on Church Street. For too many that is not the case—they are hearers of the Word but not doers. To do justly requires fair relationships in the community, especially in legal and financial endeavors. It means striving to hurt no one whether by word or deed, but rather to render to all their just due based on your relations and obligations to them. Above all, it invites Christians to do right to everyone and avoid wronging or injuring anyone.

Loving mercy refers to faithfulness and reliability. Scripture mainly uses the concept in association with covenant relationships. It invites believers to treat others with delight and charitableness. Walking with God involves obedience and humility. Biblically, to walk means to live and act in ways that emulate the patriarchs and their relationships with God. It is a summons to become so close to God that one day we can just walk on home permanently with Him as Enoch did. Why does this not happen for more Christians? Could it be because Christianity (Adventism) has become a way of life but has not been allowed to change the life, creating a dichotomy between faith as professed and faith as practiced?

Is such a disconnect normal? I say no! If we can't stand for what we believe, God can't save us. He won't take a chance that could cause sin to rise a second time. The time has come for us to know the right and not just choose it, but actually to do it. The problem James cites has escalated since Martin Luther, who identified his past with what he perceived as Paul's experience in Romans 7. The Reformer saw Paul as saying the good he would like to do, he finds himself unable to do, and the evil he doesn't want to do is what he actually does. Some take comfort in this. But is such an interpretation correct?

The time has come for Christians to stop hiding behind Romans 7:13-24. If when every time we try to do right evil presents itself, that isn't acceptable. It is sin reigning as the controlling master when Paul says that while sin may remain, it must not reign (Rom. 6:13, 14). In fact, what we encounter in Romans 7:13-24 is the Laodicean state. It is being neither hot nor cold, neither fully for God nor against Him. God cannot and will not save anyone that way. Actually, He says that He'll spit such individuals out of His mouth.

The disorder portrayed in this passage ends in wretchedness and despair. Sin has the upper hand. It is comparable to having a dead body strapped to our backs from which we can never escape. That certainly can't be the way Christian life ought to be lived. Romans 7:13, 14 may be typical for some Christians, but it certainly can't be the benchmark. It may resemble Israel's practice and Luther's, but it isn't ideal. Jesus didn't die on a cross for us to be so wishy-washy! What then is going on in Romans 7 as well as in some Christian experiences?

Basic to my understanding is Paul's own admission that he kept the law blamelessly (Phil. 3:6). Thus I see him using the "editorial 'I'" to describe what happens in a Christian experience when self assumes ascendancy. We can support such an interpretation by contrasting Romans 7:7-12 with verses 13-25. The former has eight first-person verbs and pronouns, while the latter has 38. The latter's plethora of first-person verbs and pronouns could indicate that the person depicted practices righteousness by self-effort. Certainly that isn't what Paul or James advocates; and even if they did, it would end in futility. It means that any Christian may experience Romans 7:13-24 when they have a wrong focus—whenever they take their eyes from Christ and place them on self. When Peter did that, he stopped walking on water and began sinking.

The ideal Christian experience is Romans 8, in which one is "in Christ" experiencing the Spirit-led life. Because we are adopted into God's family, no one can successfully bring a charge against us. The time has come for us to leave the false security of Romans 7:13-24. We must put faith and profession, talk and walk, together. If Sabbathkeeping is right—keep the Sabbath! Or if stealing is wrong, stop stealing! God wants us to love everybody? Then love everybody! Do we need unity in the church for the outpouring of the Spirit? Let's get united! And if prayer and Bible study are necessary to keep abiding in Christ, we should pray and study the Bible. When we read or listen to the Word, let's put in practice what we read and hear. Thank God, victory is ours in Christ!

James promises something special for those who look into the law of God—the perfect law of liberty. The law is perfect, for it is a transcript of God's character, and since God is perfect, His law would be also. Whether it references law as Torah (Genesis-Deuteronomy) or law as Old Testament Scriptures (Genesis-Malachi) is immaterial. Both contain the moral law and God's revealed will. How can James consider law as one of liberty when it contains so many restrictions? It is a matter of perspective. Most Jews saw it not as limits to keep them in but as boundaries saying thus far and no further lest you hurt yourself (*Letter of Aristeas* 139). Viewed thus, it gives liberty, not captivity. Besides, since it cannot save but shows the need of a Savior, it grants freedom in Christ.

James advocates more than just looking at the law as perfect and freeing. What he requires is remaining in and practicing the tenets it teaches. The NRSV vividly captures his sentiments. He sees those who persevere as "being not hearers who forget but doers who act" (James 1:25). Here he distinguishes between those who hear and forget and those who act on it. The latter will receive multiple blessings. They will not only be blessed in knowing that they are obedient to God but also by the pleasure they bring to others and through the joy they receive from such deeds now and the ultimate joy that eternal bliss with the Savior will bestow.

Here is a call to speak truth. But that involves more than sharing our faith and not lying. It embraces walking in truth, breathing truth, living truth, and being truth. Consider the following:

Don't be content with your Christian profession or denominational affiliation.

Don't be too pleased either if the good that you would do, you don't perform.

Be worried if you see a disconnect between profession and implementation.

For, that's not how God wants your life to be, since it's too far from the norm.

Christianity is not merely doctrines we profess.
True religion is more than rituals to perform.
Moreover, Christianity is not just belief to confess.
Religion is more than laws to which we conform.

Christianity is more than just things we do here below.
Religion is more than a lifestyle to passionately adore.
Christianity consists of more than doctrines to know.
Authentic religion is most certainly all this and more.

What then is authentic Christianity or true religion?

Being Christian is something we *be,* i.e., something we are.
True religion is a genuine state of being in this earthly region.
It's walking the walk; talking the talk, and living like who we are.

Yet to be a true Christian involves being this and much more.
It is assuredly the world's best and most genuine love affair.
It's falling in love with the greatest lover, Jesus, and Him adore
By being authentic and declaring our relationship everywhere.

—©Bertram Melbourne, July 2011

James ends this section and chapter 1 with two powerful but practical statements. The NKJV translates the first thus: "If anyone among you thinks he is religious, and does not bridle his tongue but deceives his own heart, this one's religion is useless" (verse 26). In other words, any religious claim not supported by the proper use of the tongue is inauthentic. As a recurrent theme for James, it must have been especially relevant for his readers. It is equally so for us. James infers that if by our expressions in prayers or church attendance we think we are right with God and yet we cannot control the tongue, we thereby deceive ourselves and that external profession of religion is useless. As another rendering puts it: "If anyone thinks that he is a worshipper of God and yet does not bridle his tongue, his worship is an empty thing."[2] James suggests that we can be delusional about our religious experience. Furthermore, our religious expression can be worthless and empty. That is why Paul says, "Therefore let him who thinks he stands take heed lest he fall" (1 Cor. 10:12).

In Barclay's view, James is saying, "'The finest ritual and the finest liturgy you can offer to God is service of the poor and personal purity.' To him real worship did not lie in elaborate vestments or in magnificent music in a carefully wrought service; it lay in the practical service of mankind and in the purity of one's own personal life."[3]

James's second practical statement tells us that "pure and undefiled religion before God and the Father is this: to visit orphans and widows in their trouble, and to keep oneself unspotted from the world" (James 1:27). The apostle thus defines pure religion in practical terms. Actually, he links it to social issues. Pure and undefiled religion in its expression and unadulterated form is neither so heavenly that it is of no earthly good nor so narcissistic and inwardly focused that it offends and excludes others. While worship is a God-ward expression of faith, it can't be divorced from its horizontal and relational aspects. We can't be on the up-and-up with God whom we can't see, while being less than so-so with His needy children around us.

James states that authentic religion from the divine perspective requires visiting orphans and widows in their troubles and keeping oneself unspotted from the world. He must have thought of his little brother when he wrote this. Jesus was a model of both. For example, He visited Nain to restore a son to a widow for whom his death meant loss of the last male relative in a society that defined and valued women by their male associates. Despite excruciating pain on the cross, He took time to secure His mother's welfare, thus setting an example of filial relations.

Application

Modern disciples should do no less than their Master. We should demonstrate vertical and horizontal relationships by defending the oppressed, marginalized, outcast, poor, dispossessed, powerless, and voiceless for, in the words of Martin Luther King, Jr.: "Injustice anywhere is a threat to justice everywhere."[4] In addition, we must use our voices against pornography, sex trafficking, bullying, pedophilia, family disintegration, child labor, racism, etc. Since it is for freedom that Christ freed us, not only must we not practice such ills, we must not associate with those who do, and we must boycott companies that support them in any way.

Jesus designated Christians to be the light of the world and salt of the earth. They are interesting metaphors. Light is open and visible. One can't hide it. A lamp placed under a bushel will go out for lack of oxygen. Unlike light, salt must be concealed and invisible. Yet to flavor anything, it must blend with whatever it flavors. If it is too little or absent, we notice its lack. But if it is too much, it is overwhelming and the food is useless. To melt ice or snow, salt must permeate them. Similarly, Christians can't be isolated if they are to accomplish their assigned mission.

How then can we keep ourselves unspotted from the world if we have to be part of it to influence it? It is a call to be catalysts that effect change without being transformed ourselves. The Christian must be in the world but not of it. We must not allow the world to squeeze us into its mold and dictate our actions. This means we will not accept or buy into its values and behaviors. Instead, we should allow Christ to remold our minds from within and give us strength and power to practice what we preach. The world is still saying, "We would rather see sermons than hear them." That is why we should ask God to help us take in the Word and live it out through shining as light and permeating as salt. That is authentic discipleship.

_____

[1] http://www.inforesearchlab.com/smokingdeaths.chtml.

[2] W. Barclay, *The Letters of James and Peter*, p. 61.

[3] *Ibid.*

[4] Martin Luther King, Jr., "Letter From Birmingham Jail," Apr. 16, 1963.

CHAPTER 5

Favoritism/Partiality: a Christian Response

How do we shine as light and permeate as salt? James 2 focuses on this issue. The apostle begins by attacking the problem of favoritism. Through the millennia it has had various names: partiality, prejudice, bias, bigotry, discrimination, and preferential treatment. But whatever the label, it's still the same. It is dangerous and destructive for anyone whether at the giving or receiving end. If Christians are to live what they preach and perform what they profess, how must they relate to favoritism?

James's answer is clear and unequivocal: "My brethren, do not hold the faith of our Lord Jesus Christ, the Lord of glory, with partiality" (verse 1). Since he employs the present imperative with the negative particle, it is a command to believers to stop an action already in progress. Clearly partiality existed in the church. The apostle therefore declared that it should end. He actually says they cannot hold both partiality and the faith of Jesus Christ—the Lord of glory—at the same time. The context infers they are mutually exclusive. We cannot be light and salt while favoring the wealthy over the poor and needy.

Interestingly, while James makes only two explicit references to Jesus in his letter, it teems with allusions to Jesus' teachings. James 2:1 is one of the two. He calls Jesus the Lord of glory. It could refer to His ascent to the Father and Their home in glory. "Glory" could indicate either a place or a state of being. He is the Lord who belongs in glory—that is to say, who abides in glory. The majestic sovereign of and ruler over the universe, He is the one before whom angels bow and seraphs worship. His splendor and majesty elicit doxologies. James could be saying that Jesus alone deserves preferential treatment—not the creatures He came to save. As Philippians 2:5-9 and Romans 1:3, 4 show, Jesus gave up His exalted preexistent state and took a lowered position to save and elevate us. We should reciprocate by not discriminating against others.

Jesus is the world's Savior but He is also Lord. A "lord" controls and makes decisions. Many Christians claim Jesus as Savior but not as Lord, because they want to be the decision makers of their lives. Yet Christ must be Lord of our all. We must gladly surrender to His guidance and direction. The essence of Christianity is shifting control from self to Christ. It sounds easy, but it is very hard for some. In our new elevated state we practice the ethic of Jesus that requires equality and fairness.

James is not unique with such a teaching. In the Sermon on the Mount Jesus invited listeners to impartiality in the manner of His Father who makes His sun rise on evil and good people and sends rain on both the just and unjust (Matt. 5:45). Certainly, he had heard Jesus say, "Therefore, whatever you want men to do to you, do also to them, for this is the Law and the Prophets" (Matt. 7:12). Peter also learned and taught this lesson after his Cornelius encounter (Acts 10; 11). Paul taught, "For there is no partiality with God" (Rom. 2:11). And again, "I charge you before God and the Lord Jesus Christ and the elect angels that you observe these things without prejudice, doing nothing with partiality" (1 Tim. 5:21).

Preferential treatment takes many forms. Note Mark 10:35-37: "Then James and John, the sons of Zebedee, came to Him, saying, 'Teacher, we want You to do for us whatever we ask.' And He said to them, 'What do you want Me to do for you?' They said to Him, 'Grant us that we may sit, one on Your right hand and the other on Your left, in Your glory.'" Superficially their request looks simple. But at a deeper level it implies exclusion of others and a desire for preferential treatment. That they knew what they did is evident from their approach. They sought His approval for their scheme before revealing its details. Ambitious, selfish, and power hungry, they wanted positions of prestige and clout. The right hand of a ruler denoted highest rank, and left was next to it. Together they were the highest positions of honor and power in a royal court. Furthermore, they wanted the preferred positions kept in the family.

The story shows the insensitive nature of preference from two perspectives. In context, Jesus spoke of His impending death, but they were too worried about power and prestige to hear or even care. Instead, uncaring and selfish, they sought only their own needs, not that of their peers. They wanted it all for themselves. Some people are like that. Yet Jesus didn't censure them. Instead, He showed the wrong in their request—told them what they asked was the Father's prerogative and forgave their ignorance and pettiness. It was their fellow disciples who got indignant at the request and perhaps condemned them.

When Matthew tells the story, he says their mother accompanied them and knelt before Jesus to make the request (Matt. 20:21). She came under the guise of worship to politick for her sons. Whether their mother's request is a new attempt after their initial request failed, we do not know. But although the petition came from the mother, Jesus addressed the sons in His response. He knew they were behind the proposal.

Comparing scriptures, we discover something fascinating. Three texts[1] (Matt. 27:56; Mark 15:40; John 19:25) name the women present for Jesus' crucifixion. Besides His mother, three other women are listed. All three passages name Mary Magdalene. It appears that Mary the mother of James and Joses is the wife of Cleopas. But the third woman is what concerns us here. Matthew calls her the mother of the sons of Zebedee, Mark refers to her as Salome, and John says she was the sister of Jesus' mother. It suggests that the boys' mother was named Salome and she was Mary's sister. Thus she was Jesus' aunt and they His cousins. The two brothers wanted the places of honor in the kingdom kept in the family. It shows what can happen in a church or organization when ideas and aspirations don't match or when members seek special treatment. Naturally Matthew reports that it made the other disciples angry.

We find still another text illuminating preference in a congregation. Luke 9:51-56 says Jesus' path to Jerusalem for His death on Calvary took Him through Samaritan territory. But the Samaritans refused to let Him pass through their territory. When James and John saw their reaction, they said to Jesus, "Master, do you want us to call a bolt of lightning down out of the sky and incinerate them?" (verse 54, Message). The sons of thunder wanted to burn the Samaritans, as Elijah had the captain and his 50 men also from the region of Samaria (2 Kings 1:12). For centuries Jews and Samaritans were enemies. The sons of thunder were prejudiced against their enemies and wanted to destroy them with fire. Are you so biased against another race, group, or people that you wish them dead, as the sons of thunder did?

James and John were intolerant toward those outside their in-group. John even saw a man casting out demons and stopped him because he was not one of them. Later, he asked Jesus' approval of what he had done. The Master told him, "Those who are not against us are for us." It must not be us versus them. Instead, it is we *and* us. Do you love other Christians? Do you love people not of your race, culture, clan, or country? Can we accept people who are different? The sons of thunder could not. We should celebrate differences, not censure them. The action of the Samaritans was rude. Yet rudeness does not justify crudeness. It requires understanding and tolerance. The golden rule is still applicable: "Do unto others as you would have them do unto you."

James presents a number of examples of prejudice among his readers. Note: "For if there should come into your assembly a man with gold rings, in fine apparel, and there should also come in a poor man in filthy clothes, and you pay attention to the one wearing the fine clothes and say to him, 'You sit here in a good place,' and say to the poor man, 'You stand there,' or, 'Sit here at my footstool,' have you not shown partiality among yourselves, and become judges with evil thoughts?" (James 2:2-4).

There is nothing wrong with being rich. Neither is there any defect in dressing up to go to church. We expect that visitors to church should have a hearty welcome. What then is the issue? It lies in welcoming rich people and not giving equal treatment to the poor or in giving an elevated status to rich worshippers while neglecting the poor or relegating them to a lower status. James questions the criteria employed to differentiate between the two sets of worshippers.

The apostle condemns deferential treatment to a rich person with gold rings and fine attire over against one who is poor and dressed in filthy clothes. He says that if believers should give the person in elegant garb more attention and allow them to sit in an elevated place while they put the poor individual in a lower position with reduced treatment, they have displayed partiality. Moreover, such treatment belittles and demeans those for whom Christ died.

James's scenario is not hypothetical. The rich did not treat the poor right. In fact, they were oppressing them. The church should be the place that rejects such behavior, because the ground is level at the foot of the cross. While the church ought to be a place of justice, mercy, nondiscrimination, and equal treatment. the fact that James has even to give such an exhortation suggests that such unholy snobbery had been occurring in its midst. Barclay cites documents from other early church leaders that contain similar instructions.[1]

James wanted readers to understand that such behavior is not only discriminatory and unbecoming for Christians—it is immoral. Because of who Jesus is and what He has done for us, we Christians are obligated to treat others as we have been treated. Church should be the place that puts all people on an equal footing and prohibits all discriminatory practices. Yet we are all humans who take our prejudices, faults, idiosyncrasies, preferences, etc., with us everywhere. The problem is not one of having such failures. All are sinners. The issue lies in not admitting we have them. That is to delude ourselves. God cannot save us if we cherish feelings of superiority, bigotry, pride, and preference. We must submit them to God. If Jesus, who is far superior to humans and who is the exalted Son of God, could empty Himself of all divine rights and accept the lowest form of humanity and the most degrading kind of human death to redeem us, why should we exhibit superiority that we do not really have in our relationship with others? I am amazed how Jesus, who had all, gave it up and became nothing to save us, yet we, who have nothing, want it to appear as if we have everything and treat others as nobodies!

This passage begins a deeper discussion of an issue raised in chapter 1 that is a recurring theme for James and one that must have been a concern for his readers. It relates to the agelong dilemma of the relationship between the rich and the poor. Not just an ancient problem, it daily grows more relevant. The economic gap between the two groups is not the only problem. It has related spiritual, social, ethical, and moral issues. The rich expect preferential treatment because of their status. Some Christians are not only willing to acquiesce but do so at the expense and for the detriment of the poor. That is wrong and immoral.

Beginning in James 2:5, the apostle gives his rationale for condemning prejudicial behaviors. To introduce it, he again employs a winning address: "my beloved brethren." The construction of his question is interesting. It requires an affirmative answer, thus demonstrating their acknowledgment of the fact that God has chosen the poor of the world to be rich in faith and to inherit the kingdom He has prepared for those who love Him. To nullify any perception that he implies that God chooses only poor people (especially in a context in which he emphasizes preferential treatment of the rich) James employs an ethical dative to show it is not only the poor that God selects (though He does choose poor people). Nor does the Lord give them preferential treatment. The kingdom and its blessings are for those who love God and accept and follow Him, whoever they are.

Did James say that God chose the poor of this world or the poor in the eyes of the world? The manuscript evidence is divided on this matter. One set of manuscripts gives the first reading, while another and slightly more superior set offers the latter. It appears that the latter meaning fits the context. While the readers could be seen as poor materially, it was from the perspective of the world, whose judgment is based purely on material things. Yet, as James points out, such individuals are rich in faith. They understand what dependence on the owner of a thousand hills means, and they know that while they will receive some reward in this life, the greater one awaits them in the yet future kingdom. They can give up their dependence on what exists now knowing full well their faith will not be dashed and that tomorrow's reward will be greater than today's.

That James says God chooses the poor to be rich in faith is intriguing. It echoes a teaching of Jesus. In the Sermon on the Mount He proclaimed, "Blessed are the poor in spirit" (Matt. 5:3), while in the Sermon on the Plain He declared, "Blessed are you who are poor" (Luke 6:20, NIV). Is the state of poverty a blessed one? What is it that the poor have that the rich don't? Luke tells us when he has Jesus speaking to His disciples. It implies that His disciples are the poor, because they grasp the authentic relationship between faith and possessions. They found that one has to let go of wealth to claim it in greater abundance. That's what the rich young ruler didn't get, but His disciples did. Disciples understand that God adds by subtracting and multiplies by dividing. The poor of the earth can be rich in faith, because they have given up dependence on things for reliance on Christ who is the owner of all things. As a result, they understand that an empty hand can hold more than a clenched fist.

The story of how poachers catch monkeys can apply here. Knowing that monkeys love bananas and won't let them go once they have them in their grasp, they set traps that include a banana in a container whose mouth will allow an open hand to exit but not a clenched fist. A monkey comes along, sees the banana, and puts a hand in the container to get it. Once the animal has it in its grasp, it refuses to let go. If the creature drops the banana, it can escape, but with the banana comes captivity. The monkey's love for bananas prevents it from releasing it. So it finds itself captured. Riches are like that. People tend to want more and more and to horde what they have. Thus they miss the freedom of letting it go to gain the greatest autonomy there is—freedom in Christ, something that provides all we will ever need in the present life and the greater joy of the world to come.

Some scholars think Matthew spiritualized Jesus' intent, adding the concept of blessed are the poor in spirit. Moo disagrees. He says the Greek word for "poor" has a range of meaning that includes those who are materially poor. The word can apply both to people who don't have much money as well as those who are humble and meek and who, recognizing their complete dependence on God, trust Him for deliverance.[2] Doubtlessly, both meanings are admissible here.

James 2:6 resumes the apostle's argument of verse 5, giving reasons that bias is wrong. He says that attitude dishonors the poor person, because the rich are in the habit of (1) oppressing the poor; (2) dragging them to courts of law; and (3) blaspheming the name of Christ. Christians were encountering harsh treatment at the hands of rich Jewish and pagan overlords. Such individuals seemed to have also made it extremely difficult for poor Christians. Some moneylenders and others were needlessly taking them to court. Also, some were slandering the honorable name of Jesus. Apparently some of those persons were visiting Christian worship places. Whether it was for legitimate reasons or not, we do not know. But we do know James's sentiments—that they must neither get nor do they deserve preferential treatment, and certainly not at the expense of less-affluent members.

Beginning with verse 8, James gives scriptural proof for outlawing preferential treatment. First, he goes to the law, calling it the "royal law." Any law of a king is a royal law, as we see in this sense in Esther 1:9. Since God is king of the universe, we can view His law as royal. Keener adds: "A 'royal' law, i.e., an imperial edict, was higher than the justice of the aristocracy, and because Judaism universally acknowledged God to be the supreme king, his law could be described in these terms."[3] It's also the royal law for it's the transcript of God's character, and if God is royalty, so is His law. Also, God is love. Thus if the law mirrors His character, it reflects love.

Citing Leviticus 19:18, James says that if people should honor their neighbors by loving them as self is loved, then they do well. But if they practice partiality, then the law condemns them because they would not be exhibiting love. While this includes the moral law, as his quote reveals, it seems more inclusive. It also has the Torah or whole revealed will of God in view. We can deduce this from the fact that though the Decalogue doesn't have a specific taboo on partiality, James states that if we keep the whole law and yet show partiality we are guilty of breaking the whole law (James 2:10). The injunction against partiality comes from Leviticus 19:15: "Ye shall do no unrighteousness in judgment: thou shalt not respect the person of the poor, nor honour the person of the mighty: but in righteousness shalt thou judge thy neighbor" (KJV). Furthermore, to limit it to the Decalogue would be to exclude the commands of Jesus, something we would not want to do. Thus James directs our attention to the entire revealed will of God, which includes the Decalogue.

For James to say that if we break one law we are guilty of disobeying the whole law may seem harsh to modern readers, yet a generally held view of Jewish teachers said: "Willful violation of even a minor transgression was tantamount to rejecting the whole law."[4] Not only would James's readers know this, they would also comprehend that the focus was not on the letter of the law but on its principle. If we love the Lord God with all our hearts, we will love our neighbors as ourselves. And if we love our neighbors as we do ourselves, we will not discriminate against them. Furthermore, according to Jesus' parable of the good Samaritan, our neighbor is anyone needing our help. Thus if we don't discriminate, we are observing the principle of the law and loving as God does. Also, if the law is the transcript of God's character and if God is waiting for His character to be perfectly restored in us,[5] to offend in even one point would indicate that His character is not yet complete in us. We would thus be misrepresenting Him.

That James has the moral law in mind we can also determine from the examples cited in verses 11 and 12. James refers to the seventh and sixth commandments, in that order, saying that if people obeyed one but not the other, then they would be transgressors of the law. That is why a faith response is necessary. In fact, when we accept Christ, pray regularly, nourish our Christian walk with the Word, share our faith, and always live as if in the presence of Jesus, obedience to the law becomes a natural outworking of the life. And such a relationship to law is not burdensome, as Barclay and some suppose.[6] No one can or is required to obey the law in his or her own strength. It calls for cooperation with and the aid of divine powers that are always available and just a prayer away. That is why salvation is by grace through faith and not by works—grace being God's provision, and faith being our response.

Failure takes place only on our part and thus makes us solely accountable. So James reminds us that we all will stand judged by the law. Solomon says, "Let us hear the conclusion of the whole matter: Fear God and keep His commandments, for this is man's all" (Eccl. 12:13). The writer of Hebrews adds: "And as it is appointed for men to die once, but after this the judgment" (Heb. 9:27). That is why James states that in our daily life we are to speak and act as those who will be judged by the law of liberty. Now, how can law and liberty go together? As seen earlier, to Jews law was freeing, since it showed how far we could go without hurting ourselves. It is also liberating, for it shows our need of a Savior who alone can free us from guilt.

To cap this section, James shows why we cannot afford to discriminate or be partial. He says those who do so will eventually have to answer to God. Judgment will be without mercy to those who are merciless, a point illustrated in the parable of the unmerciful servant (Matt. 18:21-35). Again, James's point is consistent with the Sermon on the Mount, in which Jesus declares, "Blessed are the merciful, for they shall obtain mercy" (Matt. 5:7). And, "Judge not, that you be not judged. For with what judgment you judge, you will be judged; and with the measure you use, it will be measured back to you" (Matt. 7:1, 2). They confirm the Christian's responsibility to be always just, fair, and impartial toward others. At the same time, we recognize that we will be treated in the same way that we deal with others. Besides, it reinforces the point that we should not be judgmental of others, since we all need God's grace. When we do judge others, we forget that when we point a finger at them, at least three are aimed back at us.

Application

A Christian response to partiality is one that deals with others as God does us and as we want to be treated—with justice, fairness, mercy, forgiveness, and love. It defends the defenseless, is a voice for the voiceless, feet for the lame, advocate for the oppressed, supporter of the marginalized, lover of the unlovely, and educator of the uneducated.

James ends with a fascinating principle: "Mercy triumphs over judgment" (James 2:13). As his brother taught, when we show mercy we'll obtain mercy. It is immaterial to debate whose mercy James has in mind—human or divine. He speaks a universal, timeless principle. Just as truth finally triumphs over wrong, so does mercy over judgment. Likewise we can conclude with the idea that those who defend the defenseless and stand for the oppressed and marginalized are displaying authentic discipleship and will triumph over those who judge and condemn others. "Compassion for the widow and orphan, manifested in prayers and corresponding deeds, will come up in remembrance before God, to be rewarded by and by."[7]

---

[1] W. Barclay, *The Letters of James and Peter*, pp. 64, 65.
[2] Douglas J. Moo, *The Letter of James, The Pillar New Testament Commentary*, online ed. (Grand Rapids: Wm. B. Eerdmans Pub. Co., 2000), p. 106.

[3] C. S. Keener, *The IVP Bible Background Commentary*, p. 694.

[4] *Ibid.*

[5] Ellen G. White, *Christ's Object Lessons* (Washington, D.C.: Review and Herald Pub. Assn., 1900), p. 69.

[6] As an example, see Barclay, *The Letters of James and Peter*, pp. 70, 71.

[7] Ellen G. White, *Testimonies*, vol. 6, p. 282.

CHAPTER 6

Dead Faith and Working Works or Dead Works and Working Faith: Either or Neither?

A small boy stood in indecision on the window ledge of a burning building. Behind him was death by fire, and before him death by a broken neck. Then he heard below his father's voice saying, "Jump, jump." He leaped right into the safety of his father's arms. What saved him—faith or works? James 2:14-26 continues to explore how Christians can shine as light and permeate as salt. It is a pivotal discussion, since many, including Martin Luther, misunderstand James. Suggesting that the apostle got it wrong, Luther rejected the book, preferring Paul. Does James teach salvation by works? For salvation, is it dead faith and working works or dead works and working faith? Is it either or neither?

James starts the unit with a thesis in the form of two penetrating hypothetical questions. "What does it profit, my brethren, if someone says he has faith but does not have works? Can faith save him?" (verse 14). The apostle presents it as an imagined dialogue between himself and a symbolic member of the community and with the book's readers as onlookers. Those viewing James as a late book by an unknown author instantly see a polemic against Paul and conclude he is deliberately repudiating the latter's doctrine of salvation by faith. A better approach is one that looks at what each says, then compares their positions. I propose that such an approach might reveal they are in agreement, not in opposition.

The question James raises is legitimate. Jesus had said twice in Matthew 7:15-20: "by their fruits you will know them." Works authenticate faith. Thus if someone claims to be a disciple and have faith yet does not bear fruit, is that claim genuine? In contrast, what about a person who displays great fruits and yet does not have faith? James says faith without works is dead, while Paul says no one will be just in God's sight by works. Who is right? Or are both of them correct despite such apparently diverse opinions? First, though, we need to answer some preliminary questions. Are they using the same definition of faith? Second, are they viewing works through the same lenses?

In James 2:15-18 James clarifies his meaning. He presents a scenario in which a disciple sees a person who is destitute of clothing and food yet accepts no responsibility, essentially asking, as did Cain, "Am I my brother's keeper" (Gen. 4:9)? Instead of clothing or feeding the individual, the disciple says for him or her to go in peace and be warmed and filled. In such contexts James says faith by itself, if it has no works, is dead—meaningless.

Let's illustrate his point. A homeowner's property became flooded. Watching the waters rise, he prayed for God's help. Finally he retreated to the roof for safety. Someone in a canoe came to rescue him, but the man didn't get in because he expected God to save him. Later a speedboat arrived to pick him up. Again he declined, believing that God would come to get him. Finally a helicopter clattered overhead. Its crew lowered a rope to pull him to safety. A third time he refused, still waiting for God. Eventually the flood engulfed his house, and he drowned. He had faith, but his works didn't match, because God had already answered his prayers with those three sets of rescuers.

A mother lived with her daughter. They received word that on a specific day Jesus would visit them. On the appointed day she wondered what she would serve Him. With her last $10 she and the daughter went to the supermarket. While returning home, they met a shabbily clad woman with obvious signs of hunger and want, carrying a baby improperly clad for the weather. Touched by the situation, the mother wanted to assist, but she had just used her last $10 to buy supplies to feed Jesus. So she handed her coat and the bag of groceries to the woman. Her daughter gave her coat for the baby, and they went home empty-handed to await their special guest.

On arrival, they found a letter in the door reading, "Thank you. Jesus." To their surprise, it had $50 attached and a quote saying, "Inasmuch as you did it to one of the least of these My brethren, you did it to Me" (Matt. 25:40). Which of those in the two stories had faith? You will certainly agree that both exercised faith. Yet what made the difference? One acted upon her faith, while the other didn't. The man died since he had faith that was by itself. It had no corresponding works. Thus it was blind faith that did not benefit him, because it did not manifest itself in action that would move him into a boat or helicopter. He did not recognize when God did come to deliver him.

On her part, the woman put her faith in action—not for salvation but in defense of the needy. She didn't say, "Depart in peace, be warmed and filled" (James 2:16). Although she had very little, when she saw someone who had less, she responded with compassion. She didn't withhold what she had. Like the widow, she gave her mite that, again like that of the widow, was her all. God rewarded her faith. The kind of faith James has in mind is that shown by the woman—belief put in action, manifesting itself in deeds done for God's needy children.

In James 2:18 he continues his dialogue with the symbolic member of the community with a discourse on saving faith: "Someone will say, 'You have faith, and I have works.' Show me your faith without your works, and I will show you my faith by my works. You believe that there is one God. You do well. Even the demons believe—and tremble!" James's symbolic protagonist argued for faith alone. They face off—one standing for faith and the other for works. The apostle calls upon his protagonist to supply the evidence for his position. But the other seems to be in a very difficult position. Faith is intangible. How do you prove the reality of a faith that does not bear fruit? How do you recognize or evaluate it? It is a sheer impossibility. Faith needs demonstration to prove its authenticity.

James counters, "I will show you my faith by my work—i.e., I will show you my faith by my fruits." The works he alludes to are what Paul calls "the fruit of the Spirit" and Jesus illustrates in Matthew 25. Paul says the fruit of the Spirit is love, which manifests itself in long-suffering, joy, peace, kindness, goodness, faithfulness, gentleness, and self-control. Jesus lists them as deeds done to the marginalized. Both sets of examples are primarily relational, affecting either our vertical or horizontal associations. Not only are they quite discernible, some are even measurable.

What intrigues me here is what I detect as a shared flaw of some Christians. They reason in fixed categories—it's either "black or white"; "this or that"; "either or"—without recognizing the possibility it could be "both and." In James it appears to be either faith or works. Barclay senses this and considers what is required here is "both and"—i.e., faith and works are both required in salvific matters.[1] While normally I concur with "both and" scenarios, I am proposing here a modified "both and" that I'll develop later.

To prove that salvation demands more than mere faith, James asks his representative opponent, "You believe there is one God?" Since it is a basic belief of Judaism, as the Shema (Deut. 6:4) shows, and an underlying tenet of Christianity, James assumes his response and moves ahead. He compliments the hypothetical person for belief by suggesting, "You do well." Nevertheless, he immediately pulls the proverbial rug from under the individual's feet, saying, "Even the devils believe and tremble!" In other words, you have not done anything unique yet. Mere belief can't be enough if even devils believe. They have an intellectual knowledge of God, perhaps even a theological one, but that's not sufficient. Though they accept that God exists, they will not be saved because they have neither submitted to divine will nor aligned their works with their belief. To surpass the devils, believers must do more than profess. They need more than intellectual assent to the notion of God and truth. Instead, they must back their profession by a fruit-bearing life.

Saving faith is more than theoretical. It is grounded in theory but backed by life-changing action. Perhaps that is what Ellen White means when she says that "prayer is the key in the hand of faith to unlock heaven's storehouse."[2] Yes, prayer is the key, but it is useless unless used in the hand of faith. To unlock the storehouse, it can't remain theory—it must become action. Faith is the hand that turns the key to get results. Theoretical faith that's not exercised and developed is what James calls dead faith. Would Paul agree? That's to be seen.

James calls his representative protagonist foolish for believing faith can be real without resulting deeds. Then the apostle inquires if his opponent wants to know that faith without works is indeed dead (James 2:20). To prove his point he presents the experience of Abraham and asks, "Was not Abraham our father justified by works when he offered Isaac his son on the altar?" (verse 21). It is an intriguing point, because Paul uses the same patriarch to demonstrate that salvation is by faith. Now, how can one use the same person to prove two diametrically opposite arguments? It is true that Abraham's actions exhibit his obedience, but was he saved by his actions or did his actions demonstrate his faith?

Then in verse 25 James moves to the example of Rahab. "Was not Rahab the harlot also justified by works when she received the messengers and sent them out another way?" Oddly the author of Hebrews, who some believe is Paul, makes the opposite claim: "By faith the harlot Rahab perished not with them that believed not, when she had received the spies with peace" (Heb. 11:31, KJV). The author clearly attributes Rahab's deliverance to faith. How then could James credit it to works? Again, which perspective is the correct one? Earlier we asked whether James and Paul are using similar vocabulary with completely differing meanings. Let's explore that notion. Are we saved by works or faith? A working faith, or a faith that works? What are the precise relationships between faith and works and faith that works? Just how should we approach the theology of Paul and of James on the issue?

Looking carefully at what James says, we must conclude that he does have an issue with *sola fide*. Yet by the same token we can see his issue is with Christians who hold such a position but for whom that's all. He has an argument with those who claim a relationship with God but whose profession and practice are inconsistent with it. His call for Christians to count it all joy when they meet various temptations sounds like some Christians in his community were complaining when their faith was tested rather than displaying Christian fortitude. His urging of Christians to ask in faith without wavering reveals that some in the church had a faith that seemed shallow and whose actions were not consistent with their Christian calling. The point of James 1:12-21 is to love God both during trials as well as when there are none. It's a summons to consistent faith whether in good or in bad times. We see such a call in verses 22-27 from a different perspective. Here it appeals to remedy the divide between word and deed, faith and practice. The discussion on favoritism calls for consistency in our dealing with all God's children. Good discipleship requires nondiscrimination in the treatment of others.

From this we can deduce that when James speaks of works, he is not using the term in the same sense as Paul did. He talks about actions that are fruits of faith, not its means. As a result, he disputes those claims of faith that are either devoid of fruits or that issue in actions inconsistent with a genuine faith walk, and instead supports one that is real, genuine, and productive. Such a walk doesn't seek to earn standing with God but to demonstrate the gospel's transforming power. It is precisely his point in James 2:22: "Do you see that faith was working together with his works, and by works faith was made perfect?" For James, faith and works go hand in hand—they are two sides of the same coin. For him, it is works that makes faith complete. Again, he is not saying it requires both faith and works for salvation. He would be the first to deny that claim. Rather, he means that saving faith manifests itself and comes to life in deeds of obedience to God and works of service to fellow humans. I see here a call to make Micah 6:6-8 practical. What does the Lord require of Christians? It is to do justly, love mercy, and walk humbly with God. Doing justly and loving mercy are the deeds for which James argues. Walking humbly with God is the faith journey. The latter thus demonstrates the former.

Further proof he isn't completely rejecting faith and is in agreement with justification by faith appears in his next sentence. "And the Scripture was fulfilled which says, 'Abraham believed God, and it was accounted to him for righteousness.' And he was called the friend of God. You see then that a man is justified by works, and not by faith only" (James 2:23, 24). He arrives at such a conclusion, because to him Abraham's faith was what led him to the faith walk with God that caused his ready obedience to offer Isaac as a sacrifice. The faith walk is foundational to obedient actions. Now, if this is James's position, is he really in conflict with Paul?

But to answer that, we must first examine Paul's background. Before his dramatic acceptance of Christianity—the religion he hated and perse- cuted—Saul was a Pharisee. Philippians 3:3-9 gives his Christian insight in and evaluation of his Jewish past that explains his presuppositions: "For we are the circumcision, who worship God in the Spirit; rejoice in Christ Jesus, and have no confidence in the flesh, though I also might have con- fidence in the flesh. If anyone else thinks he may have confidence in the flesh, I more so: circumcised the eighth day, of the stock of Israel, of the tribe of Benjamin, a Hebrew of the Hebrews; concerning the law, a Phari- see; concerning zeal, persecuting the church; concerning the righteousness which is in the law, blameless. But what things were gain to me, these I have counted loss for Christ. Yet indeed I also count all things loss for the excel- lence of the knowledge of Christ Jesus my Lord, for whom I have suffered the loss of all things, and count them as rubbish, that I may gain Christ and be found in Him, not having my own righteousness, which is from the law, but that which is through faith in Christ, the righteousness which is from God by faith."

Several things become evident from the passage:

1. Having confidence in the flesh is problematic. It is tantamount to boasting and thus places self in control. In Paul's theology the flesh is evil and is what gives sin a handle to attack.
2. He had what could have motivated confidence in the flesh—great accomplishments from a Jewish perspective—but all that paled in comparison with Jesus. So he gave them all up for Christ.
3. His parents were devout Jews. From them he inherited four things that shaped his life: (a) he had been circumcised the eighth day in keeping with the law, marking him as belonging to God's special

covenant people; (b) birth in the nation of Israel, God's chosen people; (c) he belonged to the tribe giving Israel its first king; he even had his name—Saul; (d) birth as a Hebrew of Hebrews, meaning he was an Aramaic-speaking Jew of Aramaic-speaking parents who didn't compromise by speaking Greek.

4. When he had a choice in determining his life's direction, he used his background and training to make three significant choices: a. "Concerning the law, a Pharisee." He chose to join the zealous keepers and defenders of the law. They meticulously obeyed it so that their good deeds could outweigh their bad deeds and they then could be righteous. In other words, they strove to build up merits. The law required two fasts each year, so they fasted twice weekly to acquire merit and gain standing with God. The Pharisees regarded sin as a wrong act and repentance as a right act to correct that wrong act. b. "Concerning zeal, persecuting the church." Paul was so ardent for the Pharisaic traditions and the tenets of Judaism that he saw Christians as heretics and chose to persecute them. Luke ranks his damage to the church with what a wild boar did when passing through a field (Acts 8:3; 9:1). c. "Concerning the righteousness which is in the law, blameless." His Christian evaluation of his Jewish past was that he blamelessly kept the law, but that did not gain him anything, for when he came to know Jesus he found that righteousness cannot be acquired that way.

5. The things Paul once regarded as gain, he now saw as loss and paling in significance with knowing Jesus as Lord. It also means that for him Jesus is Lord and thus is preeminent.

6. Paul counted the things he lost in coming to Jesus as rubbish. Those things were no longer paramount.

7. Paul's one desire now was to know Jesus and to be found in Him, not having his own righteousness derived from works. He wanted a righteousness originating from faith in Christ. *Here is the key point.* Paul saw the meritorious efforts of Pharisaic Judaism as self-righteous acts designed to earn favor with God but which actually led nowhere. His postconversion goal was to correct this error.

Still, he faced a problem. Based on the criteria Peter established for replacing Judas, he didn't qualify for apostleship. Though God designated him apostle to the Gentiles, some doubted its validity. It placed him at odds with some in the Jerusalem church who felt that the Gentiles had first to be

circumcised and become Jews before they could be Christians. Paul ada-
mantly opposed the idea. As a former Pharisee he saw this as a requirement
emphasizing works of law and therefore bankrupt for salvation. His stand
for salvation by faith and argument against works derives from his opposition to Gentiles or anyone else doing anything to earn salvation, since it is
a free gift of God's grace. We must see his statements on faith and works
against this background.

What is evident, then, is that Paul is not against the law but against law
keeping to gain salvation. His stance against works is not against bearing
fruit but against using it to earn salvation, something he sees as utterly impossible. It's therefore an error that believers must avoid at all costs. Note
his statement: "Therefore by the deeds of the law no flesh will be justified
in His sight, for by the law is the knowledge of sin" (Rom. 3:20). What he
says here is that no one will be declared righteous in God's sight through
observing the law, because its purpose is to give knowledge of sin—not to
save. The law reveals sin but still requires a Savior.

Romans 3:21 resolves that problem when it declares, "But now the
righteousness of God apart from the law is revealed, being witnessed by
the Law and the Prophets." How can it be apart from the law and witnessed
to by the law? It is revealed apart from the law as a means of salvation—i.e.,
law-righteousness. God's righteousness can't be bought or sold. Neither
earned nor merited, it is a free gift of God's grace. Paul says it is witnessed
to by the law and the prophets. The Hebrew Scriptures has three sections:
the law, the prophets, and the writings. When Scripture employs any two of
the terms, it means the whole, so that when Paul says it is witnessed to by
the law and the prophets, he is saying his doctrine of righteousness by faith
agrees with the entire Hebrew Scriptures.

The two introductory words of verse 21 are very significant. In Romans
1:18-32 Paul shows that Gentiles need righteousness. Next, in Romans 2:1
to 3:8 he establishes that Jews also must have it. Finally, in Romans 3:9-20
he points to the universal requirement for righteousness. Thus the whole
world stands guilty before God. He then begins verse 21 with "but now."
Opposite to universal guilt and need is God's provision of righteousness.
Divinely given apart from any works of law, it is consistent with the Hebrew Scriptures. Where did this revelation of God's grace take place? At
Calvary through Jesus' sacrificial death. Thus the cross stands at the center
of history, dividing those saved by faith in a Messiah to come and those
saved by a Messiah who has come. The sins of those prior to the cross were

forgiven but not dealt with until Jesus' death (Rom. 3:24-26), and future sins have already been dealt with at the cross. It takes faith from both sides. But how does the apostle use the term *faith?*

A good example is Ephesians 2:8, 9: "For by grace you have been saved through faith, and that not of yourselves; it is the gift of God, not of works, lest anyone should boast." For Paul, grace is God's provision in Jesus' sacrificial death. Faith is the human response/acceptance of God's offer. For Paul, salvation can't be self-earned or works-achieved—it is a free gift of divine grace. Humans won't have cause to boast. No one will go to heaven and challenge God with the claim that they earned the right to be there by their righteous deeds. This is what the apostle means in Romans 3:27: "Where is boasting then? It is excluded. By what law? Of works? No, but by the law of faith." Law in this context means "principle." Paul says that the principle of faith rules out any boasting, because salvation is by means of faith, not of human effort. He further clarifies this in verse 28: "Therefore we conclude that a man is justified by faith apart from the deeds of the law."

What is evident therefore is that James and Paul may be using the same vocabulary but not with the same meaning. For Paul, faith is the means of salvation. It is a trusting relationship in which the believer is "in Christ Jesus," a state that is salvific. In this kind of relationship one becomes adopted in the family of God and manifests the fruit of the Spirit. Paul does not consider works as fruit of this kind of relationship. Rather, speaking from his Pharisaic past, he addresses works as what one does to gain standing with God and thereby salvation. Thus they are taboo, because no one can successfully earn their way to the kingdom. As we have seen, James addresses a faith that we can call "mere" faith—a claim to salvation that is not demonstrable, or if it is, is not acceptable Christian conduct. For him, works are the fruits of faith. Thus I see Paul and James in agreement with each other and not in opposition, as some claim. In fact, Paul even states that we are God's workmanship created for good works (Eph. 2:10).

We now need to resolve whether salvation is by dead works and working faith or dead faith and working works. Is it either or neither? Dead works from James's perspective are bad and cannot save. That is also true of dead faith. Working works from Paul's outlook is also unable to save. What then can save? A faith that works! Earlier, I suggested that while Barclay argues for a position that recognizes both faith and works ("both and"), I would propose a modified "both and" posture. I say modified, for while it is clear that Paul and James would see both as involved in the process, I would have to assume a modified position, since the two aspects are not equal copartners. What I mean is that faith is most assuredly the means of salvation, and while saving faith must redound in good works, they do not have equal roles. We are not saved by both faith and works. Neither is faith itself a work. Instead, we are saved by faith that demonstrates its heavenly connection through good works. My modified position, then, is that we are saved by a faith that works. Works demonstrate the authenticity, genuineness, and proper grounding of faith.

Application

Faith without works is dead. And works without faith is equally so. We need a faith that works—one that is vertically grounded and horizontally connected. A faith that proves its genuineness by feeding the homeless; that visits the sick and cares for orphans, widows, victims of HIV/AIDS, fatherless children, and the imprisoned; that mentors others; that clothes the naked; that gives voice to the voiceless; and that defends the marginalized. Do we need such disciples in the twenty-first century? Most assuredly! It is the best way to shine as light and permeate as salt, for people would rather see a sermon any day than hear one.

---

[1] W. Barclay, *The Letters of James and Peter*, p. 73.

[2] Ellen G. White, *Steps to Christ* (Mountain View, Calif.: Pacific Press Pub. Assn., 1956), p. 94.

CHAPTER 7

Counsels to Would-be Teachers: Stewardship of the Tongue

In James 3:1-12 the apostle revisits the issue of curbing the tongue, which he had raised earlier (James 1:19, 26). It must be a key concern to him. Here he may have a specific group in mind. "My brethren, let not many of you become teachers, knowing that we shall receive a stricter judgment. For we all stumble in many things. If anyone does not stumble in word, he is a perfect man, able also to bridle the whole body" (James 3:1, 2). Gay Byron is correct in seeing a link between proper use of the tongue and the teaching profession.[1] I agree with Longenecker[2] that, when viewed from the positive, James is making an affirmative statement about the tongue. Teachers will receive stricter judgment for their use of their tongues owing to their pivotal role in lives and society. Because of that, they need to display proper stewardship of the tongue.

Teachers use their tongue continuously. It is the principal instrument for their vocation. Thus it is imperative for them to regulate their speech carefully. A few years ago, while traveling in another country, I met a former student. As we talked about what she presently does, I learned she no longer attended church or professed a religion. It puzzled me, considering her Christian piety, passionate love for God, and the great promise she had shown in the past. As I explored what had transpired, I found she started down that path because of a chance remark another professor had made in a religion class. When she took the inopportune remark to its logical conclusion, it destroyed her love for and belief in God. That is why James states that it is a mistake for those not having good stewardship of the tongue (and he says that's most of us) to seek the teaching profession.

Apparently teaching was a desired profession in James's day, one with great honor.[3] James tries to deter some from entering it by presenting some of its challenges. First, teachers will receive a stricter judgment—to whom much is given, much is expected. Perhaps that is because of the dual ability of the tongue, a point he will make later. Those who do not stumble in words can bridle the whole body, exhibiting self-control. Teachers use words, and if one cannot bridle one's tongue, teaching is the wrong profession. Inability to exercise stewardship of the tongue and wanting to teach are as mutually exclusive as a person who hates to see blood desiring to be a surgeon.

The word "bridle" in verse 2 recalls its use in James 1:26 and anticipates the comparisons of control he'll employ from nature and shipping. While in James 1:26 the tongue was to be bridled, here the requirement is not limited to it, as the "also" implies. It covers the entire body. Robertson correctly observes that the implication is the person who bridles the tongue "does not stumble in speech and is able also to control his whole body with all its passions."[4] While it is a seemingly small and insignificant part of the body, James suggests that it has a lot of influence and needs ordering. Note the images he employs to illustrate his point.

First: "Indeed, we put bits in horses' mouths that they may obey us, and we turn their whole body" (James 3:3). James 1:26 called for Christians to bridle their tongues, but James 3:2 admitted that it is a difficult task for most of us. The author says bridles are put in horses' mouths. To ensure that no one misses his meaning he employs a purpose clause to indicate the rationale for such an action. It is to achieve obedience and manipulation of the horses' whole bodies to alter their direction. "The body of the horse follows his mouth, guided by the bridle."[5] So the call for us to bridle our mouths is one to let them be guided by the positive control of the bridle. The bridle for us is a Christ-controlled conscience. Failure to bridle the tongue would thus allow the body to follow the mouth in any direction it chooses. That's not good for disciples.

Second is the example of a ship. "Look also at ships: although they are so large and are driven by fierce winds, they are turned by a very small rudder wherever the pilot desires" (James 3:4). The contrast here is between the immensity of the vessel and the small size of the rudder that controls it. Martin fascinatingly proposes that such rudders were tongue-shaped.[6] Such a possibility adds to the aptness of the imagery and readies the readers familiar with it for the application to the human tongue. Ships seeming so large to James pale in size compared to our modern cruise liners. Back then large ships ranged from 100 to around 240 feet long by 79 feet wide (the latter being Caligula's Lake Nemi ships—floating palaces). The largest ship of

James's time may have been Caligula's barge, which measured between 95 and 104 meters (341 feet), with a beam of about 20.3 meters (66 feet). Six decks high, it carried a crew of 700-800. Today's largest cruise ship, Royal Caribbean's *Oasis of the Seas,* is 1,187 feet by 208 feet, with 16 passenger decks that house more than 6,000 passengers.

Yet the principle remains the same—a small rudder controls the movement of a vessel that's much larger than itself. James's application says, "In the same way, the tongue is a small part of the body. But it brags a lot" (verse 5, NIrV). His point is that by directing the movement of the ship someone has charge of the rudder. Similarly, the tongue needs control so that it doesn't say whatever it chooses on its own volition.

James's point is quite clear. Neither bridle nor rudder masters itself. Each needs external guidance. Horsemen control the bridle, and the rudder requires a pilot or captain. Likewise the tongue is as small as both bridle and rudder. In an adult male it weighs 2.5 ounces. It should not be allowed to have its own way. Yet some people allow their tongues to blabber away wildly. They speak and then think rather than think and then speak. James says such individuals should be neither teachers nor supervisors. In those positions they create more harm than good. That's why tongues need bridles. Relevant then, his counsel is still applicable today. Too many speak irresponsibly whether complaining about leaders or criticizing others. Not only does it create discord—it can destroy character and sap energy needed to fulfill mission.

Germane is the question of who should control the tongue. Here is where the illustrations collapse, for while external controls are necessary for inanimate bridles and rudders, the tongue is part of a living being that contains an internal controlling mechanism—the mind. That's why James calls on Christians to bridle their tongues. The tongue is a small organ and should not control us—we must master it. Yet by his own admission anyone who doesn't offend in words is perfect. Why is control of the tongue so hard if humans are expected to tame it? Because of self—the root cause of sin. Humans want to control themselves and others but cannot effectively do it because of sin and its consequences. The unaided human mind is prone to evil. Good (spiritual) things don't come naturally or easily. That is the point of Romans 7:13-23—self in control preventing execution of the good we want but allowing the evil we don't want. Paul attributes it to resident sin—sin remaining and reigning. So, as with bridle and rudder, we need external regulation. That is precisely the indwelling Spirit's role. Here

Romans 8 and its themes of "in Christ," "no condemnation" experience, "adoption into the family of God," and a Spirit-led life become relevant.

James turns next to a natural phenomenon metaphor. "Think about how a small spark can set a big forest on fire" (James 3:5, NIrV). Then, as now, forest fires began by carelessly thrown sparks or through lightning. Even the sun shining through pieces of glass can spark them. Anyone living in such forested areas as the western United States, Australia, and the Western Cape of South Africa fully grasp this imagery. The apostle's use of it indicates that it was familiar to his readers. It takes only a spark from an improperly discarded cigarette or match to set a fire going that can destroy thousands of acres of forestry and homes. The metaphor contrasts the size of the spark with the vast damage created and again readies the reader for its application to the tongue.

"And the tongue is a fire, a world of iniquity. The tongue is so set among our members that it defiles the whole body, and sets on fire the course of nature; and it is set on fire by hell" (verse 6). Some consider it as a difficult passage to translate.[7] Another interpretation renders it as "The tongue is a fire, a world of iniquity is the tongue among our members."[8] Yet another says, "And the tongue is fire; in the midst of our members the tongue stands for the whole wicked world." The image of the tongue as fire is common among Jewish writers.[9] We should not stumble at the fact that he says the tongue is a fire, for the spark is itself fire albeit in miniature. Through the image of the small spark and its resultant damage James declares that a small tongue ignites large social infernos. It aptly describes the potential for ruin, irrepressible nature, reach, and influence of the tongue. Yet how is the tongue a world of iniquity?

Robertson sees James as implying that it can play havoc among the members of the human body.[10] Yet how is it able to do that? Davids observes that "the sense is simply that since speech is the hardest faculty to control it is there that one first observes 'the world' in a person's heart. Jesus made a similar observation (Mark 7:14-23 par.). As in the teaching of Jesus, James states that the tongue stains the whole body."[11]

"The tongue is the point of entry for the world's greatest evils," Richardson adds. "Its boasts inspire multitudes to evil, especially the words of false teachers. Thus, whether inside or outside the church, the wickedness of the world is an immense blaze set by the little fire of the tongue. The tongue is 'the world of evil.' In the ancient way of thinking, this is not a difficult phrase. The body was the microcosm of the universe. In all its complexity, the human being was a small, self-contained universe, thus the term 'microcosmos.' There is a double sense of microcosm here: not only the body in relation to the universe of nature but also the tongue in relation to the universe of wickedness. Thus, contained within the tongue or speech are all the representations of wickedness in the world. . . . The power of verbal representation is not slight; this James knew full well. Words have the power to elicit action; indeed, the activity of speech itself interprets every other human action. There is no evil act that the tongue cannot tell, let alone initiate."[12]

Fires of anger, backbiting, contention, criticism, cynicism, doubt, envy, fear, jealousy, joking, murmuring, rumor, strife, lying, and talebearing ignited by the tongue can devastate both individuals and whole communities. A will under Satan's control can destroy harmony, peace, and community. It is in the sense of its relation to the devil and the damage that such a tongue can cause that James says it can ignite the fires of hell. Here is more reason to tame the tongue by being "in Christ" and placing it under His discipleship.

All he said so far about the tongue notwithstanding, James still sees need for more. It suggests that the problem was extremely pervasive, the damage very grave, or a combination of both. At any rate, he begins another comparison based on another natural phenomenon. "For every kind of beasts, and of birds, and of serpents, and of things in the sea, is tamed, and hath been tamed of mankind: But the tongue can no man tame; it is an unruly evil, full of deadly poison" (verses 7, 8, KJV). While human beings can domesticate or control all kinds of creatures, they cannot tame their own tongue. Why is that so?

James offers a rationale. The tongue, he declares, is an unruly evil full of deadly poison. He compares the issue of the tongue (words) with the venom of a deadly snake. Both can cause death. "That is, it acts upon the happiness of man and the peace of society, as poison upon the human body."[13] James seemed to have paraphrased Psalm 140:3: "They sharpen their tongues like a serpent; the poison of asps is under their lips." In the context of Psalm 140, those whose tongues are full of deadly poison are evil. One would not expect such a condition in the church where we should have converted Christians—joint heirs of Jesus—who have been adopted into God's family. But if it does, it calls for a new experience with Jesus and a change of heart.

James now shows how unruly and poisonous the tongue can be. "With it we bless our God and Father, and with it we curse men, who have been made in the similitude of God. Out of the same mouth proceed blessing and cursing" (James 3:9, 10). The implication is that we would not want to do anything other than bless God, yet we think nothing of cursing our fellow human beings, forgetting that they are made in God's image. Thus we actually disrespect that image and glory as reflected in humanity.

It reminds us of the Passion Week. Whether James had it in mind isn't clear, yet the point is that we should not rely on the crowd or its opinion, for it is fickle. The same ones that on Sunday shouted, "Hosanna! 'Blessed is He who comes in the name of the Lord!'" (Mark 11:9) on Friday shouted, "Crucify him, crucify him" (Luke 23:21, KJV). The same tongue that speaks well of someone one day might also defame that individual on another. We see such duplicity further pictured when James says that "out of the same mouth proceed blessing and cursing."

It is fascinating what James does here. While he has been reasoning that the tongue is an unruly and uncontrollable member, the illustration does not say that the tongue blesses God and curses other humans. It says that *we* employ it to bless God and curse our fellow humans. Obviously the tongue does not speak on its own. Jesus declared that "a good man out of the good treasure of his heart bringeth forth that which is good; and an evil man out of the evil treasure of his heart bringeth forth that which is evil: for of the abundance of the heart his mouth speaketh" (Luke 6:45, KJV). The tongue only reflects its owner's state of the mind (remember that the ancient world considered the heart what the mind is for us today). The tongue speaks what the heart thinks. What some of us may need, then, is mind surgery—not by a neurosurgeon but by the Great Physician.

Thus James doesn't address his rebuke to the tongue but to its owners. "My brethren, these things ought not to be so" (James 3:10). In other words, this must not continue. "It is a moral incongruity for blessing and cursing to come from the same mouth."[14] Also, Jesus commanded His followers to bless those who cursed them and to pray for those who misused them (Luke 6:28). How could they resort to cursing others on the one hand and combining blessing and cursing on the other? Yet the tongue itself can neither understand the rebuke nor make the needed adjustment. Its owners must perform those tasks. But neither can they know to do them or succeed in making the changes on their own. It requires a power outside of and beyond self.

James offers other reasons that blessing and cursing should not proceed from the same lips. It is not representative of the natural order of things, as he seeks to point out through a series of rhetorical questions. "Does a spring send forth fresh water and bitter from the same opening?" (James 3:11). While he does not expect an answer, James shows what its nature would be if given. The Greek construction requires a negative response. Thus if that wouldn't happen in a spring—a thing—it should not occur with the minds and tongues of persons with brains. Thus a pure heart and a lawless, cursing, uncontrollable tongue are mutually exclusive.

"Can a fig tree, my brethren, bear olives?" (verse 12). Then, as now, they grafted plants, but only similar plants will survive. We can graft together different types of oranges but not fig trees with olive trees. They do not belong to the same kind. Likewise with grapes and figs. They have nothing in common—like must produce like, the same principle as in the first illustration. If it is true in the agricultural world, it is equally so in the spiritual realm. Just as we can't serve God and mammon, we can't combine the works of the flesh with the fruit of the Spirit. God must be Lord of our all or He'll be Lord not at all. We must not miss James's point in this section: "Bad things don't produce good things. And so a person who is not right with God and walking daily in his presence cannot consistently speak pure and helpful words."[15]

To end the section, James reverts to the illustration of the spring, saying none of them yields salt and fresh water at the same time. It must be one or the other. Similarly, a disciple can't have an evil tongue and a pure heart. Nor can one bless God and simultaneously curse His children. Since horses are controlled for effective work, and ships to make their destinations safely, the tongue must be regulated to do good for God and humanity. Therefore, control your tongues!

Application

How do we apply this lesson to the contemporary church? Today everyone wants to teach and especially preach. Shepherding God's flock has gotten increasingly difficult. Everyone thinks they know how to do a better job than pastors trained for the job. Things have deteriorated such that a recent book is titled *Clergy Killers: Guidance for Pastors and Congregations Under Attack*. The message of James is still relevant—"let not many of you become teachers" and "bridle your little tongue." I think it is binding on all of us, both leaders and followers, to be careful in the use of our tongues. Leaders should not lord it over God's heritage. The flock should neither consume the pastor for Sabbath or Sunday lunch nor be disrespectful in their words. We all will one day give an account to God for the use of our tongues. Let's bless and not curse others.

During my more than 40 years in ministry I have made a few interesting observations: 1. Some people detest in others what they dislike about themselves. 2. Many project onto others what they themselves are thinking and not only attribute that motivation to them but blame them for it. 3. The people on church boards, trustee boards, and church committees who are most vociferous against sinners and what they see as wrong in others most often are covering up something in themselves, assuming that if they speak out against others they will themselves escape scrutiny. But the Good Book is still true: "Love covers a multitude of sins" (1 Peter 4:8, NASB) and "Be sure your sin will find you out" (Num. 32:23). 4. We all need to watch our tongues.

Thus my counsel is this: If you have nothing good to say about another, it is better to remain silent than share the stories you have made up about that person or those someone else has shared with you. Your turn will come one day, and it will be measured to you as you measured to others. I would also advise you that something is wrong if you must speak ill of others or their motives for you to look good. If you end up doing so, you will not be the only one to know what you are doing. For what goes around comes around! So be a good steward of your tongue!

---

[1] In Brian K. Blount, gen. ed., *True to Our Native Land: An African American New Testament Commentary* (Minneapolis: Fortress Press, 2007), p. 466.

[2] R. Longenecker, *Patterns of Discipleship in the New Testament*, p. 238.

[3] W. Barclay, *The Letters of James and Peter*, p. 79.

[4] A. T. Robertson, *Word Pictures*, vol. 6, p. 40.

[5] *Ibid.*

[6] Ralph P. Martin, *James*, Word Biblical Commentary (Waco, Tex.: Word Books, 1988), p. 105.

[7] Robertson, vol. 6, p. 42.

[8] *The SDA Bible Commentary*, vol. 7, p. 526.

[9] Barclay, *The Letters of James and Peter*, p. 85.

[10] Robertson, vol. 6, p. 42.

[11] P. H. Davids, *The Epistle of James*, pp. 142, 143.

[12] Kurt A. Richardson, *James*, electronic ed., Logos Library System, The New American Commentary (Nashville: Broadman and Holman Pub., 2001), p. 152.

[13] *The SDA Bible Commentary*, vol. 7, p. 526.

[14] Robertson, vol. 6, p. 45.

[15] D. J. Moo, *The Letter of James*, p. 166.

CHAPTER 8

Wising Up:
Wisdom in Speech and Life

James 3:13 presents a bold rhetorical challenge: "Who is wise and understanding among you? Let him show by good conduct that his works are done in the meekness of wisdom." The question "Are any of you wise and understanding?" (NIrV) implies that, then as now, there were those who felt that they were wiser and more understanding than others and could do things better. Rather than condemning or refuting their claim, James challenged them to prove it. Talk is cheap, as we often say. So do more than mere talk—show it—is what I hear him saying. Yet James decided to set the parameters for that response: "Show it by your conduct." He aimed at the would-be teachers he had addressed in verse 1.

James queries whether they had the wisdom to be practical teachers, an idea found in the Greek word *sophos*.[1] He also has another group in view, one that he describes with the word "understanding" (*epistamai*). They claimed expert status and scientific skill and even felt superior.[2] Charles Erdman calls them "self-appointed teachers" who were more interested in defending their positions and defeating their opponents than in establishing truth.[3] Such wisdom is earthly, demonic, and sensual (verse 15). Also, there is a difference between knowledge and wisdom that many often miss. While knowledge involves comprehension of facts, wisdom is the ability to use that knowledge appropriately. For James true wisdom is a gift whose source is God.

Since talk is cheap, James challenged such would-be teachers to demonstrate their truth by their conduct. The Greek word he employed indicates more than just behavior. Implying one's way of life, it involves more than haphazard occurrences of good conduct and denotes the whole pattern of what we do. The NIrV brings out the notion of the tendency of the life and not the intermittent good deed with its reading: "You should show it by living a good life." It follows up by adding, "Wise people aren't proud when they do good works." They do everything "in the meekness of wisdom" (NKJV). What is the meekness of wisdom? Robertson calls it a startling combination.[4] Barclay[5] says the Greek word used for "meekness" has no English equivalent. He cites Aristotle, who defines it as "the mean between excessive anger and excessive angerlessness." Further, he sees it as depicting the person whose feelings and emotions are under perfect control. It is the temperament of the one in whom everything is mixed in the right proportions.[6]

Such an attitude seems to emanate from and is rooted in heavenly wisdom. Obtained through dependence on the Spirit, it is meek and humble, because it knows and relies on its divine source. Those possessing it do not do their works to be noticed but because they are the right things to do and will glorify God. James here presents the positive attributes of a God-endowed and God-directed teacher.

Yet he also implies that the hearts of some of the would-be teachers were bitter with envy and self-seeking. The NIrV labels the traits as "jealousy" and "bitterness" (see verse 14). James declares that those who possess them should neither boast nor lie against the truth. It implies that a sure way to verify whether someone has true wisdom is to see if they display arrogance. Humility and meekness characterize the posture of the God-endowed teacher; boasting and a sense of superiority embody that of earthly would-be teachers. A truly wise disciple is kind, forgiving, understanding, giving, compassionate, tolerant, gracious, and filled with God's love.

How does one lie against truth? First, perhaps those who are jealous and bitter deliberately do not speak the truth. They lie against it because they misrepresent it, since such traits are not consistent with truth. The second way to fathom James's thought is to see its link with Jesus, who said, "I am the way, the truth, and the life" (John 14:6). From that perspective, it means those who lie against the truth actually lie against Jesus, who is the truth. Either way, since such traits are alien to Him, to claim to know Him or be His follower while exhibiting them is to lie against Him.

Now, if we claim to be followers of Jesus, then our actions not only represent Him but imply they would be His own actions. To display un-Christlike traits is thus to falsify Him. Jesus said, "By this all will know that you are My disciples, if you have love for one another" (John 13:35). The various divisions created by the work of would-be teachers conflict with this principle and misrepresent the teachings of Jesus.

But James doesn't stop here. "This wisdom does not descend from above," he further states, "but is earthly, sensual, demonic" (James 3:15). Such "wisdom" is all talk and devoid of action. Sensuous, it appeals to the basest instincts and impulses of the individual. Barclay calls it a characteristic of the natural person.7 It pinpoints for Jesus' disciples the three areas of their greatest struggle: the world, the flesh, and the devil. The world seeks to "squeeze [us] into its own mould" (Rom. 12:2, Phillips). We shouldn't get our motivation or dictates from it but must instead allow Christ to control our minds. To achieve that we must saturate our mind with the Word.

On the night of His arrest Jesus told His disciples a truth that modern disciples must not forget: "Watch and pray, lest you enter into temptation. The spirit indeed is willing, but the flesh is weak" (Matt. 26:41). At times we know what is right and desire to do it but end up failing. Jesus gives the reason here—the flesh is weak. Since the entrance of sin, the unaided natural human inclination has not been to the truth and right. That's why we need cooperation with the Divine. Jesus exemplified it in His life and ministry. He was victorious through constant communion with and dependence upon His Father. Should we expect to do any less? That's why He advises that we guard the avenues to the soul ("watch") and pray. The primary avenues to the soul are the sense organs that lead to the brain. We must be careful what we allow to pass through them, because, as they say in the computer world, "Garbage in; garbage out." That's why we must guard what we see, taste, smell, touch, and hear. We may think we're in control and know when and where to stop. Yet we must not forget that "fools rush in where angels fear to tread." Peter supposed he was in control and swore he'd never forsake Jesus. But a few hours later he denied knowing Jesus three times. "The spirit indeed is willing, but the flesh is weak" (verse 41).

The devil knows our weaknesses, even if we think we have none or that he has no idea what they are. As we learn from Jesus' temptations, Satan strikes at our weakest moments, quotes Scripture, and even impersonates angels of light.[8] Instead of appearing with a pitchfork or in forms many of us might expect, he may come as a parent, a child, a friend, a relative, a coworker, a boss, a spouse, a sibling, or in other astonishing ways. Ellen G. White tells us, "Jesus was victor in the second temptation, and now Satan manifests himself in his true character. But he does not appear as a hideous monster, with cloven feet and bat's wings. He is a mighty angel, though fallen."[9] We should never underestimate him to our own peril or give him access whether through doubt, fear, or what we listen to, read, touch, or watch. Always we must guard the gateways to our minds.

As we have noted, James labels the would-be teachers' wisdom as devilish or demonic. Such descriptors link it to its true source—Satan, our archenemy, who determines to ensnare us. "Your adversary the devil walks about like a roaring lion, seeking whom he may devour," Peter reminds us (1 Peter 5:8). They say that only sick or wounded lions wander about searching for prey. Healthy lions lie in the tall grass by water holes and let their prey come to them. When the animals approach to drink, they look for lions before beginning. Then as they get complacent after drinking, the lion roars, creating panic among the animals. The ensuing confusion allows the beast to attack. The devil is a wounded lion. Jesus has already defeated him, but he runs around, desperately trying to catch prey. Since we know his intent, we should foil his attempts. What he advocates should not be named among or be identified with Christians. It is contrary to the divine nature and thus inconsistent with genuine Christian practice.

James 3:16 appropriately observes, "Where envy and self-seeking exist, confusion and every evil thing are there." Both involve an attitude often found in some churches and organizations called factious rivalry. It often has its source in the same motivation that led to the first sin—desire for personal gain. Frequently it cleverly hides among those who nourish it until it's too late. Lucifer had said, "I will ascend into heaven, I will exalt my throne above the stars of God; I will also sit on the mount of the congregation on the farthest sides of the north; I will ascend above the heights of the clouds, I will be like the Most High" (Isa. 14:13, 14). It took Calvary to expose his true motives.

The first sin was rooted in self, and that still lies at the base of every sin. Not only are selfish ambition and factiousness rooted in selfishness, it's at the center of divisive and destructive behavior. We aren't jealous or envious of others unless we compare ourselves with them and assume that they are ahead of us in some way or have something that we want. Adultery, for example, results when we desire for our own selfish satisfaction someone who belongs to another. Nor do we covet another's possession until or unless we decide that it must be ours. Self is also at the core of stealing and murder. Let's decide not to follow the devil's footsteps and to guard against his wiles. It requires self-control and constant connection with our only source of help—Jesus.

Envy and self-seeking have other side effects. They produce "confusion," i.e., disorder that comes from instability.[10] When people take sides, the resulting discord leads to schisms and factions. If not monitored and appropriate measures taken, the meeting could end in disaster. Not only does James 3:16 support such a view, but so do the events at Corinth that Paul describes in 1 Corinthians 1:10-4:21. The cunning, charm, and subtlety of the would-be teachers, and those like them, require wisdom, divine guidance, and the Spirit's leading to deal with them. Church leadership needs to be alert to prevent disaster. James suggests here that where envy and self-seeking abide, every evil thing resides. Clearly the characteristics of such false "wisdom" would disqualify those who possess it for any teaching environment—ancient or modern, school or church. What we see is the outworking of the wisdom of the world.

Christian leaders need therefore to saturate their environment with prayer and the Word. They must exorcise worldly wisdom so that Christ can enter and divine wisdom make its home. Where Christ resides, the devil or his imps can't abide. Note: "But the wisdom that is from above is first pure, then peaceable, gentle, willing to yield, full of mercy and good fruits, without partiality and without hypocrisy" (James 3:17).

The characteristics that James outlines here set heavenly wisdom apart from the earthly version. Such traits would be in demand in any organization and desirable in any good teacher. Those who possess them would thrive in a church setting or a school environment. It is evident that those having them are gifted by the Holy Spirit and are in union with divine agencies. Looking at some of the qualities listed could prove helpful for disciples and teachers. James says those who have such wisdom will be pure. Barclay comments that those who would approach the Greek gods would have minds that thought holy thoughts. That is, they were devoid of ulterior motives and self-interest.[11] The next characteristic is peaceable. The root word here—"peace"—implies that heavenly wisdom or those with it will promote peace. Contrary to popular belief, peace is not necessarily the absence of strife. Having the Hebrew shālōm in mind, it indicates a sense of knowing that all is well in our relationship with God and that He is our friend. Such vertical connections naturally have horizontal dimensions that enrich and empower people's interpersonal relationships and make all they do be the result of love.

Another characteristic is gentleness. We can also render it "equitable."[12] One person calls it "sweet reasonableness."[13] The NIrV's translation succinctly summarizes the other traits for us, "It obeys. It is full of mercy and good fruit. It is fair. It doesn't pretend to be what it is not" (verse 17). All of them are wonderful traits to possess and practice if we want to be in the business of eternity preparation and kingdom building. Through the years, as I have worked with youth and in education, I have discovered that of the traits youth hate in a teacher, leader, or pastor, hypocrisy or pretense heads the list. They want us, and God expects us, to be genuine and sincere. Let's not disappoint them.

James 3 climaxes with a highly profound statement: "The fruit of righteousness is sown in peace by those who cultivate peace" (verse 18, HCSB). It states that the outcomes of justice emanate from peace and are found in those who cultivate peace. Some people appear to thrive on conflict or contention. They seem to hate peace. James says, on the contrary, there are those who cultivate peace and sow seeds that bear fruit in righteousness. I believe that here is where all Jesus' disciples should be. Love and peace should lubricate all their actions and interactions. In conclusion then, let us chart the differences between the two wisdoms.

Worldly Wisdom	Heavenly Wisdom
bitterness	pure
envy	peaceable
self-seeking	gentle or equitable
boasting	willing to yield/approachable
lying	full of mercy
earthly	from above
sensual	merciful
demonic	produces good fruits
confusion	is not partial
every evil thing	without hypocrisy/sincere

What seems evident is that the two lists are not random. Some thought clearly went into them. James wanted to be sure that his readers would avoid those characteristics that would bring dishonor to Christianity and to espouse those traits that would make them better citizens here while at the same time qualify them for citizenship above. Modern Christians can benefit from them too.

James 4 introduces a new discussion on issues already raised relating to the tongue and earthly wisdom. Several things indicate the connection. First, the references to conflicts, disputes, and war echo the fires caused by the tongue. Second, in James 3:13, 14 the apostle asked for the fruits of the life to indicate the possession of wisdom, and in verses 14-17 he contrasted two kinds of wisdom. Now in James 4:1, 2 we encounter the results of earthly wisdom. Third, in James 3:17, 18 James spoke of the peaceable nature of heavenly wisdom and noted that a harvest of righteousness is sown in peace by those who make peace. Here, in James 4:1, 2, we see conflicts, disputes, and wars, things that are the direct opposite of peace. The implications of the rhetorical questions of verse 1 that follow on the heels of James 3:17, 18 are that the characteristics he notes all find their source in unspiritual and devilish earthly wisdom (James 4:15, NRSV).

The Greek words used in James 4:1 are pregnant with meaning. For Robertson, "war (*polemos*...) pictures the chronic state or campaign, while *machē* . . . presents the separate conflicts or battles in the war. So James covers the whole ground by using both words."[14] It indicates the seriousness of the allusions James makes to what was transpiring in the church. After the apostle asked the source of those wars and conflicts, he then himself answered through another question: "Don't they come from the cravings that are at war within you?" (verse 1, HCSB). It implies that the external wars reflect internal ones. People battle others to appease the struggles raging within themselves. Perhaps this notion helps to substantiate an earlier allusion that people detest in others what they do not like in themselves. Now we can say they are even willing to fight about it.

The ethical character of the problem is not visible in the English translations but is unmistakable in the Greek. The word employed for "cravings" or "pleasures" is *hēdonōn,* from which we get our English word "hedonism" and the modern playboy philosophy with its focus on self, pleasure, and the sensual side of life. Again, it highlights the role of self and desire in sin and conflict in the church. James says their origin is not heavenly wisdom no matter how pious, wise, and well-meaning their advocates may try to appear.

"You desire and do not have," James continues. "You murder and covet and cannot obtain. You fight and war. You do not have because you do not ask. You ask and don't receive because you ask with wrong motives, so that you may spend it on your evil desires" (verses 2, 3, HCSB). The passage further accentuates the fact that desire is at the root of evil and self at the base of all sin. The apostle uses murder and covetousness as representative sins and shows they emanate from desire to gratify self. We covet because we believe someone else has what we should have, and when we can't obtain it, we will even murder for it. James says that some will even wage war to get what self desires, emphasizing the chain effect or progressive nature of sin.

The passage highlights still another problem for some Christians: they compare themselves with others. For example, they may pray and get their blessings but remain dissatisfied, because it seems that what they receive is less than that of their neighbors. Rather than looking inside to find the problem, they resent and hate their neighbor. Some see a Santa kind of God and ask for little things, which they receive. Others visualize a big God and make their requests accordingly and are rewarded. But that angers their neighbor. Next James puts his finger on yet another difficulty. Some don't receive because they don't ask, for we have to ask to receive, and we have to seek to find (Matt. 7:7).

Other Christians complain that their prayers never get answered. Apart from the fact that some do not recognize the answers to their prayers is James's notion that others ask with the wrong motive and so don't receive. And what is that wrong motive? "That you may spend it on your evil desires" (James 4:3, HCSB), i.e., asking to gratify and/or glorify self. Well, then, what is the right motive? It is honoring God's name, building His kingdom, and benefiting His needy children. As for those unable to see God's answers to their prayers, why are they so blind? We pray for patience, for example, but what is patience? As we have already seen, it is endurance under trial. When in answer to our prayers God sends the trials that will help develop the patience we sought, we complain.

As a young minister I had someone in my life whom I encountered daily who tried my patience and my faith. I recognized that to withstand it I had to learn to love the person. Yet every time I prayed for help to love the individual, the next day the person's attacks would intensify. Only then did I begin to understand the nature of endurance under trials. It is also true that sometimes God's response comes so swiftly that we fail to recognize it. A woman who did not have the money to pay her rent prayed and asked God to send help. As she opened her eyes, she heard a knock on the door. Paralyzed with fear, she wondered if the landlord had come to collect the rent. She knelt there and would not go to the door. A week later she met an elder from her church who told her God had impressed him to take her some money. But no one opened her door. The answer to her prayer had knocked, and she had turned him away.

Thus far James has saturated his epistle with loving address, especially at strategic points. But now the apostle shocks his readers with another kind of approach. He calls them adulterers. The label could indicate church members guilty of literal adultery, something not surprising in light of his usage of a form of *hēdonōn* twice in the previous verse. It could also refer to those engaged in idolatrous practices, as implied in his comments about the love of wisdom, pleasure, the world, and self. If the latter, we know that idolatry is spiritual adultery.

Now he follows up with "Don't you know that friendship with the world is hostility toward God? So whoever wants to be the world's friend becomes God's enemy" (verse 4, HCSB). It suggests spiritual adultery is included, an understanding further reinforced by verse 8. There he refers to the double-minded, an allusion to a statement he has already made (James 3:12) and one that reminds us of Jesus' statement that we cannot serve both God and mammon. The truth is that the world's manner of operation, philosophy of life, and way of thinking are incompatible with the Christian's. While the world is fixated on self and pleasure, the Christian focuses on God and service. The approaches are mutually exclusive. Again, the old adage is still true: "God must be Lord of our all, or He will be God not at all." Thus Jesus said long ago, "No one can serve two masters; for either he will hate the one and love the other, or else he will be loyal to the one and despise the other. You cannot serve God and mammon" (Matt. 6:24). If one selects the world, one thus becomes God's enemy. The converse is equally true. If we choose friendship with God, that automatically makes us an enemy of the world. There is no middle ground, especially when spirituality is concerned.

James 4:5 is a difficult verse. We find no scriptural passage saying that explicitly. The best way to view it is as a follow-up to verse 4. God will not share affections. He says He is a jealous God—"You shall not bow down to them or worship them; for I, the Lord your God, am a *jealous* God" (Ex. 20:5, NIV). The Lord has every right to that claim, because He's our Creator, Sustainer, Redeemer, and Guide. We should not interpret jealousy in anthropomorphic terms. Rather, it means that nothing or no one is comparable to Him. False gods are human creations, and things are inanimate. When we worship or place anything on the same plane as the Lord, it brings Him down on the same level with things and demeans Him. Let's worship God and God alone and allow Him to remain in the lofty heights to which He belongs.

Yet we can view the passage in still another way. Since we can't serve two masters and since God wants all our affections, the text could be saying that a Christian's friendship for the world "grieves the 'jealous' Spirit of God, who seeks our undivided affections. Man's jealously is selfish; God's jealousy reflects simply His intense concern for the welfare of His children."[15]

James follows up with an encouraging notion for Christians: "But He gives more grace" (James 4:6). To assure the undivided attention of His children and ensure they understand His love for them, God showers them with more and more grace. Jeremiah says: "Through the Lord's mercies we are not consumed, because His compassions fail not. They are new every morning" (Lam. 3:22, 23). God has made provisions for all our needs, but we need to claim them. They are ours just for the asking. The humble and contrite Christian will receive grace without measure, while the proud who choose their own way or that of the world won't. God has no alternative but to reject the proud. At any rate, God's gifts for His children far surpass what anyone can offer, but this requires undivided attention.

How can we demonstrate our repudiation of friendship with the world, rejection of the earthly worldview, acceptance of heavenly wisdom, and alignment with God? James addresses this in the last four verses of this section with 10 imperatives:

1. Submit to God—the essence of sin is living a self-directed life, while the Christian life is a change of center from self to God. It involves submitting self to divine control.

2. Resist the devil and he will flee from you—here is an invitation to take a stand against Satan. Too many yield without resisting. But standing up to him brings immediate results. He will flee. Christ has already wounded and defeated him. He's a wounded lion trying to impress, but he can't withstand opposition or challenge. Resist him and let him run!

3. Draw near to God, and He will draw even nearer to you. Not only must we submit to God and resist the devil—we need to get close to the Lord. That is the surest guarantee of successful discipleship. And how do we approach God? Through prayer, Bible study, Christian witnessing (the best way to keep your faith is to give it away), and always living as if in His very presence. As we do those four

simple things we will develop a deepened and life-transforming relationship with Him. It is also true that the devil won't tarry near those who are close to God.

4. Cleanse your hands, you sinners—to achieve and maintain intimacy with God, one must have clean hands and a pure heart (Ps. 24:3, 4). The psalm's imagery depicts the external cleansing vital for ritual purity.

5. Purify your hearts, you double-minded—as already noted, the ancients viewed the heart as the seat of the emotions, what we today call the mind. Not only did the Old Testament require ceremonial cleansing but purity of mind, implying ethical purity. Intriguingly, James makes his demand of those who were double-minded or whose loyalties weren't stable but split between the world and Christ.

6. Lament—recognition of our true condition leads to contrition. Given what James has described since James 3:13, we see a need for affliction of soul, and that is what the Greek word he employs here pictures.

7. Mourn—with *theos* as part of its root, this is a call to godly sorrow or repentance. True contrition requires tears.

8. Weep—as those who sow in tears will reap with joy, so those who weep in true repentance will be rewarded, for godly sorrow receives forgiveness.

9. Let your laughter be turned to mourning and your joy to gloom—a call for those who once enjoyed hedonic pleasures now to turn the laughter they derived from them to mourning as they recognize their true condition and its resultant end.

10. Humble yourselves in the sight of the Lord, and He will lift you up—true disciples know they are creatures and thus products of the hand of a mighty Creator before whom they need to stand in awe. The normal human tendency is to self-exaltation and pride, but before the heavenly monarch contrition and humility is the only appropriate response. And it brings a reward. According to James, the ultimate outcome is divine exaltation.

Application

We have seen that true disciples need to recognize their responsibility for judiciously using the tongue in teaching and other discipleship settings.

True discipleship also involves controlling the tongue and not letting it run unrestrained, since it can create irreparable damage. James's counsel applied not only to his day—we need it as much in our time of free speech and constitutional rights. While such rights are real and applicable to all, true disciples accept their responsibility to God and their obligations to their fellow beings, because we are our brother's and sister's keeper.

Finally, authentic disciples reject earthly wisdom and treasure the heavenly kind that will make them loving, lovable, and kind in their horizontal connections and submissive, humble, and trusting in their vertical relationships. Thus we will find a difference in their speech and life.

[1] A. T. Robertson, *Word Pictures*, vol. 6, p. 45.

[2] *Ibid.*

[3] In Roger Ellsworth, *James* (Leominster: Day One Publications, 2009), pp. 116, 117.

[4] Robertson, vol. 6, p. 46.

[5] W. Barclay, *The Letters of James and Peter*, p. 91.

[6] *Ibid.*

[7] *Ibid.*, p. 93.

[8] See E. G. White, *The Desire of Ages*, pp. 118-120.

[9] *Ibid.*, p. 129.

[10] Warren W. Wiersbe, *The Bible Expository Commentary* (Wheaton, Ill.: Victory Books, 1989).

[11] Barclay, *The Letters of James and Peter*, p. 95.

[12] Robertson, *Word Pictures*, vol. 6, p. 47.

[13] Barclay, *The Letters of James and Peter*, p. 95.

[14] Robertson, vol. 6, p. 49.

[15] *The SDA Bible Commentary*, vol. 7, p. 532.

CHAPTER 9

Discipleship of the Mind

While in high school, I discovered the following quote attributed to Sir Isaac Watts. Not only did it fascinate me, it became a mantra:

"Were I so tall to reach the pole, or grasp the ocean in my span, I must be measured by my soul: the mind's the measure of the man."

Watts undeniably spoke a truth, because Jesus said, "A good man out of the good treasure of his heart brings forth good; and an evil man out of the evil treasure of his heart brings forth evil. For out of the abundance of the heart his mouth speaks" (Luke 6:45). What proceeds from our mouth can reflect the state of our mind. That is why we need to think carefully before speaking. Thus discipleship of the mind is imperative for us to be authentic disciples. James now resumes his dialogue on stewardship of the tongue and reintroduces a theme he had left behind in James 3:12. With a prohibitive imperative he commands: "Do not speak evil of one another, brethren" (James 4:11).

The persistent repetition of prohibitions concerning speech or involving the tongue is significant, as is the use of the present imperative with the negative particle. Collectively they speak to the condition of those whom James addresses. Singularly they say something is going on that needs to stop. The Greek usage calls for the community to stop something they were doing. It says that they are in the habit of speaking evil of each other. To what does James refer? It is to "utterance of false charges that defame another person's reputation."[1] "Those who meet in corners and gather in little groups and pass on confidential tidbits of information which destroy the good name of those who are not there to defend themselves."[2]

Have you ever had someone say to you, "I am telling you this only because you are my friend. I trust you. No one else knows this, and you are the only one I am telling. If I hear it again I know it is you"? Gossip is one way of slandering a person. Barclay calls it malicious gossip and notes that it usually occurs in the absence of those being talked about. He says it is a sin characteristic of the unredeemed and unsparingly condemned by the Bible.[3]

That it was happening among church members, especially those of a Jewish background who knew that the Old Testament prophets condemned it, is shocking. Yet despite this, James calls the offenders "brethren" in his usual endearing way. He uses the word "brethren" not only to refer to the males in the congregation but inclusively to designate both sexes. Although he disapproves of their conduct, he values them as fellow saints, believers in a shared cause, and devotees of a mutual Savior. It presents a striking contrast. The "brethren" may be slandering each other but James is affirming them, treating them with respect, and demonstrating a discipleship of the mind that reveals itself in stewardship of the tongue. And while the behavior certainly deserved harsher condemnation, he shows restraint.

He does not stop there, however. "He who speaks evil of a brother and judges his brother, speaks evil of the law and judges the law" (verse 11). Since we can sum up the whole law as loving God supremely and our neighbor as ourselves, then those who criticize fellow disciples break the law, since they are not loving when they treat His child unkindly. Moreover, those who behave in such a way actually love self more than neighbor. They display a superior attitude that Scripture condemns.

How can we love our neighbors as ourselves and yet speak critically or spread slanderous evil about them? I see one of three options here. We either do not love self, do not love our neighbor, or perhaps love neither self nor neighbor. A lot of pain that some people suffer derives from hatred of self and lack of self-respect that reveals itself in disrespect of others. Others hate themselves because they believe they are not as pretty or as talented or as blessed as those around them. They vent their anger on those they assume are pretty, gifted, or blessed. It explains why we must not compare ourselves with others. Christ is the standard and the one with whom we should evaluate ourselves by.

Not only shouldn't we speak disparagingly or slanderously of others, we should not even listen to such stuff. It actually wastes precious time that we could devote to God, His Word, or accomplishing His mission. Such conduct created the sin problem in the first place. Satan began his rebellion using slander and gossip. By the time one third of the angels and Eve realized what was happening it was too late. That's why we must be careful.

Ellen G. White says that church members "can exert a strong influence if they will cease their gossiping and devote their time to watchfulness and prayer."[4]

One person I know of treats gossip and slander in a fascinating way. She says to the speaker, "Have you said that to X? If you have not, know that if you don't, I am going to tell them. I am sure you would rather do it yourself than have me do it for you. That's the Christian thing to do and is what Jesus recommends in Matthew 18." Needless to say, gossipers stay away from her. Why not emulate her? God is depending on you, my friend! Yet, how does one who slanders a fellow believer judge the law? Does that make sense?

Barclay observes, "Now, if a man breaks a law knowingly, he sets himself above the law. That is to say, he has made himself a judge of the law. But a man's duty is not to judge the law, but to obey it. So the man who speaks evil of his neighbor has appointed himself a judge of the law and taken to himself the right to break it, and therefore stands condemned."[5] It seems that James is saying that such a person elevates self above the law. Rather than being subject to and obeying the law, that individual deliberately chooses to disobey it and has by that very action assumed a position above it. It is tantamount to deciding what should or shouldn't be obeyed. That very action involves a judgment about the law.

An insightful writer adds, "By disregarding the law's jurisdiction over all men the critical faultfinder aspires to be a lawmaker rather than a lawkeeper."[6] No human is really able to do such a thing. Whoever attempts it already stands condemned, knowingly or unknowingly, by the very law they seek to judge. James makes this exact argument at the end of verse 11: "But if you judge the law, you are not a doer of the law but a judge." Since the first lie in Eden, humans have tried to assume prerogatives that are not theirs.

Now this becomes further problematic. Which human, apart from Jesus—and we know He is the God-man—can meet the qualifications required for being a judge in spiritual matters? No one! Paul agrees. Quoting Psalm 14:1-3, he says: "There is none righteous, no, not one" (Rom. 3:10). James also concurs. "There is one Lawgiver, who is able to save and to destroy. Who are you to judge another?" (James 4:12). God is the only one in a position to judge. Not only is it true from the theological perspective—the apostle even employed the Greek construction to aid him in making the point. He used the word *heis*, which excludes all but God.[7] Only He is knowledgeable enough to determine expertly and errorlessly the motives and character of others. He is Creator, Sustainer, Redeemer, and ultimate Judge. Omnipresent, omniscient, omnipotent, unchanging, eternal, just, forgiving, righteous, holy, and immutable, He knows our thoughts and motives. God alone can read unspoken thoughts. Since no human is competent enough to discern between truth and error, right and wrong, the saved and unsaved, Jesus said that we should leave judgment to God. Yet some Christians in James's day, and others today, dare to assume divine prerogatives. Yet things are not always what they seem to be, as the following illustrate. What do you see?

Musician or girl's face? Which do you see?

Do you get the point? Your perspective is not the only one. How can we judge another when we do not have all the facts? That's why we must leave judgment to God.

That's not all that's wrong here. The one who speaks ill of a neighbor and thereby judges the law goes again Scripture, which does not support such behavior. God said: "Whoever secretly slanders his neighbor, him I will destroy" (Ps. 101:5). Jesus said: "Judge not, that you be not judged" (Matt. 7:1). Again, God declared: "Vengeance is Mine, I will repay" (Rom. 12:19). Ellen G. White adds: "Be careful how you speak. Be careful how you represent the religion you have accepted. You may feel it no sin to gossip and talk nonsense, but this grieves your Saviour, and saddens the heavenly angels."[8] James's community should have known better; and certainly contemporary Christians ought to do even better, since we have the witness of both Testaments.

Moreover, such an attitude breaches a command Jesus gave His disciples before departing. A fundamental distinction between disciples and the world is love. Jesus said, "By this all will know that you are My disciples, if you have love for one another" (John 13:35). The church is a family. Families are characterized by love. So when we deliberately label people by categories that divide or exclude, or that present images of disunity, we misrepresent what Jesus expects for the church. Distinctions such as liberal, conservative, Black, White, Hispanic, African, rich, poor, educated and uneducated, islander and mainlander that are exclusive rather than inclusive distort the spirit of Jesus' command, because they are not based on, nor do they promote, love. Authentic disciples always create and support things that promote peace, harmony, and love.

With James 4:13 the author moves to another issue requiring stewardship of the mind. He addresses those who seem *not* to understand they are not in full control of their lives and actions. Subject to a higher power who alone is responsible for such major decisions, we need stewardship of the mind to aid proper self-evaluation and to exercise wisdom when making plans. Thus James admonishes, "Come now, you who say, 'Today or tomorrow we will go to such and such a city, spend a year there, buy and sell, and make a profit'" (verse 13).

Does that mean we should not think out what we want to do in the future or keep a calendar? Is strategic planning for churches, businesses, and individuals hereby tabooed? Absolutely not! In fact the text does not even say the itinerant teachers and businesspeople shouldn't consider where to go. That is not the issue. Pictured here are individuals who globe-trot to peddle their wares. Although they claim to be Christians or at least lovers of God, they do not include Him in their plans. They act as if they are in control of their lives and destinies. The goal is to make money and get rich—they have no thought of God or fellow human beings. We can see here those who are self-assertive, self-confident, self-assured, self-motivated, and self-centered. Their plans may be precise, expansive, calculated, and tight. Yet they lack something fundamental. Many in our postmodern, I-centered, anything goes, materialistic generation need to listen to James. Friend, there is more to life than travel, pleasure, making a living, merchandizing, and laying away for tomorrow, as important as they are. None of us got here by chance. Life is not an endless road to nowhere. There is a Designer, an ultimate cause.

To help his readers grasp this and develop stewardship of the mind, James declares, "Whereas you do not know what will happen tomorrow. For what is your life? It is even a vapor that appears for a little time and then vanishes away" (verse 14). James says that unlike the might, permanence, omniscience, and sustaining power of God, humanity is limited, transient, and powerless. Not only do we not know the future, our lives are like vapor—here now and gone the next minute. Instead of arrogance and self-assurance, what we need is the prayer of Moses: "So teach us to number our days, that we may gain a heart of wisdom" (Ps. 90:12). What James emphasizes here and wants his readers to remember is the tentative nature of human planning. We are not our own but are subject to a higher authority no matter how powerful and superior we may assume we are. The parable of the rich farmer perfectly illustrates the point.

"The ground of a certain rich man yielded plentifully. And he thought within himself, saying, 'What shall I do, since I have no room to store my crops?' So he said, 'I will do this: I will pull down my barns and build greater, and there I will store all my crops and my goods. And I will say to my soul, "Soul, you have many goods laid up for many years; take your ease; eat, drink, and be merry."' But God said to him, 'Fool! This night your soul will be required of you; then whose will those things be which you have provided?'" (Luke 12:16-20).

James does not leave us in doubt about what an acceptable approach to the issue should be. He cautions, "Instead you ought to say, 'If the Lord wills, we shall live and do this or that'" (James 4:15). Given the uncertainties of life, this is a plea for submission to God. It is a clear call for Him to be in the picture, especially when we ponder the realities of life. He is saying that we shouldn't be so smug. Because we can't make it alone, we must pause to seek help. There's One who truly loves us and truly wants to help. Give Him a chance. Don't boast in your evil, James tells us. Such boasting is arrogant and will not get us anywhere. We must submit to God!

James closes the chapter using words that I will never forget. The speaker at my college baccalaureate service intoned them from an unforgettable translation. "He that knoweth to be extraordinary and remains ordinary, to him it is sin" (see verse 17). James is saying, in the matter at hand, what needs to be done is known, and since it is, then do it. To do otherwise is to be liable and accountable.

Application

How does James's message apply in the twenty-first century? Is it still relevant? I think it is just as vital today as when first given. Some might think it is more needed than ever. Stewardship of the tongue and discipleship of the mind are still in demand. Many excuse themselves by saying, "They know that that is how I am. I tell it as is and call it as I see it, and I don't care." But it does matter. Too many Christians speak and then think rather than the reverse. As a result, too many, especially the young, get needlessly hurt by such attitudes and positions. And we need to remind ourselves that it displeases Jesus when we injure any of His little ones (Matt. 18 and its parallels).

Contemporary Christians also need to learn to resist the devil so that he will flee. Many think they are invincible and can choose to stop their bad habits whenever they choose. But they are on dangerous ground, not knowing or underestimating the enemy. It is too late in the game now for that. To survive, I recommend the following recipe:

2 cups of family worship
3 cups of prayer spread out evenly
2 cups of private devotion and personal quiet time with God
4 cups of praise
1 cup of sharing
10 heaping tablespoons of patience
½ cup of kindness well interspersed and mixed in

Mix thoroughly, and then place all ingredients into a human mind for cogitation and implementation.

The postmodern, fast-paced, Internet-surfing, digital social network generation may not think they need God, but it must learn from the parable of the rich farmer and would do well to listen to James, who counsels that life is a vapor. You see, life does not consist of the number of toys we have, the size of our bank account, how much of the world we have visited, how far up the corporate or academic ladder we have climbed. Instead, live so that your life will make a positive impact on others, because, believe it or not, someone is being influenced by your life for good or bad. Let's make it be for the positive.

None of us knows what is going to happen in the next minute, not to mention tomorrow. Furthermore, many find out that there is indeed Someone who is in control of our destinies when it is too late to change the course of their lives. Don't let that happen to you. Ultimately, this chapter presents seven traits to avoid:

1. Speaking evil of another
2. Judging others
3. Judging the law
4. Living arrogantly
5. Making material gain your sole aim

6. Boasting

7. Knowing good and not doing it

Solomon's conclusion is still correct: "Let us hear the conclusion of the whole matter: Fear God, and keep his commandments: for this is the whole duty of man" (Eccl. 12:13, KJV) Let us heed this good advice and remember that to whom much is given, much is expected, and that he "who knows to be extraordinary and remains ordinary, to him it is sin." Let us pray this prayer that can help us be extraordinary and give us the stamina to endure:

"God grant me the strength of character to keep God in my life and put His interests above mine. Lord, grant me the strength of will to curb my tongue. Help me not to sit in judgment on others or the law. Grant me wisdom to act from integrity, not from expediency.

"So help me God!"

---

[1] Walter A. Elwell and Philip Wesley Comfort, *Tyndale Bible Dictionary*, Tyndale Reference Library, 1206 (Wheaton, Ill.: Tyndale House Publishers, 2001).

[2] W. Barclay, *The Letters of James and Peter*, p. 111.

[3] *Ibid.*

[4] Ellen. G. White, *Testimonies*, vol. 2, pp. 246, 247.

[5] Barclay, *The Letters of James and Peter*, p. 111.

[6] *The SDA Bible Commentary*, vol. 7, p. 533.

[7] A. T. Robertson, *Word Pictures*, vol. 6, p. 54.

[8] Ellen G. White, *Fundamentals of Christian Education* (Nashville: Southern Pub. Assn., 1923), p. 457.

CHAPTER 10

Unjust Practices for Christians: Keeping Wealth Under the Belt

A story tells of a farmer who prayed to God for a blessing. Appearing to him in a dream, God promised to bless him on condition he agreed for his immediate neighbor to have a double portion of what he got. Reluctantly he accepted the condition. First, he asked for 100 dairy-breed cows to enhance his business. God answered his prayer, and the man was extremely happy until he looked over the fence and saw the 200 his neighbor now had. For his second wish he requested new barns, a milking facility, a tractor, and two trucks to transport milk to the depot. Again, he was pleased until he discovered that his neighbor had received twice as much. When the Lord arrived for his final wish, the farmer asked to be blinded in one eye. The selfish, hard, and unkind heart of His child grieved God. Christians ought not to be like that.

Yet James 5:1-6 details some egregious practices of the rich. The verses reflect another return to a topic already discussed but which the apostle repeats again and again. "Come now, you rich, weep and howl for your miseries that are coming upon you!" (verse 1). "Come now" is an attention grabber that James loves. We need to answer two questions before proceeding. First, how does the warning here compare with that in James 4:13? Second, does the apostle have a problem with rich people or just their wealth?

To the first, we say that the discussion in James 4:13 concerns those who chase affluence so acutely they forget God in the process. Their sole aim is wealth. They climb through, crawl under, run over, jump on, and knock down anything in their way to it. James invites them to pause a moment to consider the cost. Conversely, James 5:1-6 treats the affluent as a category. They have already acquired wealth and have had opportunities to use it to bless others but refuse, choosing instead to hoard it for their own selfish ends.

Second, if he does not have a problem with the rich or their riches, why does he talk so much about them and return so often to the subject? If he does, what's wrong with them? Or is James favoring the poor, as many of us seem to do, buying into a philosophy that suggests the church will always consist of poor people who'll always be with us? Some believe that because the poor have nothing else, they accept religion, but those who have wealth do not need it.

Those who subscribe to such a philosophy either misunderstand Scripture or are deliberately trying to distort it. Jesus made the remark in a specific context (Matt. 26:11 and parallels). It neither says that the church will always attract the poor nor that it will always consist of the poor. Nonetheless, because of greed and other expressions of selfishness, the world will continue to have the poor. However, Jesus was not giving a decree, prediction, or prophecy about the church's composition, as the context illustrates. Mary had just used an expensive jar of perfume to anoint Jesus' feet. Surmising its cost and how it would benefit him, if placed in the disciples' treasury, Judas objected but tried to camouflage his real motive by saying the money could have been better spent to help the poor. It could be that others may have also shared that sentiment not knowing his real intent.

At any rate, knowing Judas' motives were impure but not wanting to expose him publicly while still validating the honor Mary had just given Him, Jesus made His statement. What He meant was that they should not question the investment made on His behalf by using the poor as a foil. For while there will always be the poor in the world to support, He would not always be here to be honored. Jesus was alluding to His impending death. The focus was on the contrast as it related to the brevity of the remainder of His stay and not on the poor and the permanence of their situation. James understood this and thus did not have a problem with the rich.

If indeed the apostle had a problem, I think it was with the attitude of the rich, their contempt for the poor, and their lack of insight about the true nature, purpose, and function of wealth. By not sharing, they miss the blessings of wealth in the here and now and are in danger of losing the happiness of the hereafter. James was not scolding, castigating, ostracizing, or berating the wealthy for being rich—rather, he was advising them on what riches could do to them and of the impending judgment that was certain to accompany their choice. What is significant here and in life generally is that while we are free moral agents who make our own decisions, consequences always accompany our choices. James lays out some of them here for all to see.

And what are some of the consequences that he presents? First, weeping and wailing. Why such emotion? It would be the rich's way of coping with their impending misery. While the wealthy often looked with scorn on the poor who reciprocated with envy, James actually reversed the roles here. He heaps scorn and condemnation on them for their improper choice and use of their possessions.

James informs his readers that while their riches served as their security, they would not endure to support them. Their protection would vanish as their wealth rotted, their clothes would become moth-eaten, and their gold and silver would be corroded. Barclay says that the ancient world apparently had three sources of wealth,[1] and James lists them all here. First, there were flocks, grain, fruit, wine, and oil.[2] Most of them are perishable, and they are the ones James describes as wealth that would rot. Their shelf life was limited anyway.

Second, expensive and elaborate clothing seemed to have been a principal way of displaying affluence in biblical times generally and James's day particularly. One only has to remember Achan's stealing of a Babylonian garment at Jericho. A change of clothing was the payment Samson offered for solving his riddle and was one of the lures that caused the downfall of Gehazi after the healing of Naaman. After all, many peasants had only one garment.[3] One author notes that extravagance in dress and clothing was one of the excesses at the time of Jesus' birth, and that the clothing of John the Baptist served as a rebuke.[4] James announces that such splendid garments, once signs of wealth, would soon become cause for grief. They would provide food for moths or be targets of their destruction. The contrast is striking. The rich wouldn't use them to help sustain the poor but now they would be sustenance for insects. Yet Jesus died for people, not moths. People often brag about their rise from rags to riches but here James pictured the descent from riches to rags, all because people have not yet learned that blessings are not given for hoarding but for sharing. God told Abram a long time ago, "I will bless you and make your name great; and you shall be a blessing" (Gen. 12:2). This is still true.

Third, the biggest sign of wealth, currency—gold and silver—would also be affected by the approaching judgment. Then as now, society regarded them as precious metals. James says they would corrode. We know that silver corrodes and coins rust. But what he implies here is that even such valuable and desirable metals would not be safe from the divine judgment upon the selfish rich. It is important to note that currency or things in constant use do not corrode or tarnish. The imagery then is one of misuse. Rather than employ their God-given wealth to bless others, particularly the poor, the rich hoarded and stored it for a future day, allowing deterioration. Not only will corrosion occur, it would act like a poison or cancer and would not only testify against them but would eat their flesh like fire. The rich will face judgment for their unjust and unholy practices. Whether this refers to judgment in this life or to the eternal judgment is immaterial— both can happen for the unrepentant rich who abuse the poor and needy, and the latter will take place anyway.

Continuing his denunciation of the wealthy, James says, "You have hoarded wealth in the last days" (James 5:3, NIV). This translation suggests that James felt they were living in the last days. Despite this, the wealthy were not utilizing their means to the best ends. Instead of using it in the interest of those in need and/or to spread the gospel, they persisted in laying away treasures, forgetting that Jesus said, "Where your treasure is, there will your heart be also" (Matt. 6:21, KJV), and "Do not lay up for yourselves treasures on earth, where moth and rust destroy and where thieves break in and steal; but lay up for yourselves treasures in heaven, where neither moth nor rust destroys and where thieves do not break in and steal" (verses 19, 20). I have never seen anyone who was able to take and use their wealth in the grave. Archaeology has shown the fallacy of the idea of being buried with possessions, servants, etc. Those Egyptian tombs that survived plundering still had their objects untouched and unused. It reinforces the need to take seriously the instructions that we must make our preparation for the afterlife *now* and that it involves how we treat others and where we place our treasures.

We see this idea further illustrated in James 5:4, in which the apostle cautions the rich about how they treat the workers in their fields: "Look! The wages you failed to pay the workers who mowed your fields are crying out against you. The cries of the harvesters have reached the ears of the Lord Almighty" (NIV). James asks the rich to give him their attention, as though he had not already had it, indicating that what comes next is of utmost significance. He confronts the dishonest gain achieved through failure to pay workers. But what he envisions here is not a one-time or even an occasional failure to pay, though he would not condone that. Rather, he uses the perfect tense. It pictures an action that was in progress in past time, has come to a stop, but still has continuing consequences. This would imply that some would still have unpaid wages, while others would still suffer the visible effects of its loss. Still others could be still struggling with obvious signs of want and/or their depressed state of body or mind.

The Greek text says the rich did not withhold wages because of a temporary inability to pay but kept them back fraudulently. Yet the Hebrew Bible is quite clear on this matter. First, the Pentateuch says, "You shall not oppress a hired servant who is poor and needy, whether one of your brethren or one of the aliens who is in your land within your gates. Each day you shall give him his wages, and not let the sun go down on it, for he is poor and has set his heart on it; lest he cry out against you to the Lord, and it be sin to you" (Deut. 24:14, 15). Again, "You shall not cheat your neighbor, nor rob him. The wages of him who is hired shall not remain with you all night until morning" (Lev. 19:13). The prophetic books also weigh in on the matter: "Woe to him who builds his house by unrighteousness and his chambers by injustice, who uses his neighbor's service without wages and gives him nothing for his work" (Jer. 22:13).

No wonder James comes out so strongly against the behavior of the rich. The greedy and self-centered rich exploited their farmhands while enriching themselves, but the abused workers were crying out against the injustice. Those were not ordinary protests—they were pleas for justice and vengeance. James gave good news to the exploited but bad news for the greedy exploiters. He said their cries had reached the ears of the Almighty. Such cries never go unanswered, for the Lord has said, "Vengeance is mine, I will repay. . . . It is a fearful thing to fall into the hands of the living God" (Heb. 10:30, 31, NRSV), as tender, merciful, forgiving, and just as He is. Yet, because of God's forgiveness, grace, and mercy David would much rather fall into divine hands than human ones. But God's grace and mercy won't last forever. He will be the judge and will repay the unjust and the wicked. Then it will indeed be "a fearful thing to fall into the hands of the living God." It is advisable to make our peace with Him now.

James's outrage reached its crescendo in James 5:5 with "You have lived on earth in luxury and self-indulgence. You have fattened yourselves in the day of slaughter" (NIV). It is absolutely amazing and totally horrifying as well as unconscionable that while the rich withheld the wages of their employees and acted fraudulently toward them, they were themselves living in luxury, satisfying their own self-indulgence in sensual living. Both Jews and Gentiles regarded such behavior as intolerable, and it should have been especially so for Christians. No one with a conscience should treat others the way the wealthy acted toward the poor.

In some way it reminds me of the parable of the prodigal son. Thinking only of self, he requested his portion of the family estate while his father still lived. To do that implied that he wished his father dead. Besides, in those days, people rarely converted property into cash. They kept it in the family if at all possible. Leaving home, the younger son threw himself into sensual living. He took no thought of God or fellow humans. Yet he soon discovered a significant truth that James teaches in this chapter and that all wealthy people need to know—namely, riches are fleeting and wealth has wings. Before long, his riches went and with it also his friends. Soon one who had been on top of the world found himself at the proverbial bottom of the barrel, stealing food from pigs, an animal that Jews should not even have been touching. Providentially he came to himself before it was too late. That does not happen for everyone and therefore why we need to approach life from the right perspective.

The rich addressed by James apparently did not discover it in time. To illustrate their situation, James said they were fattening themselves in the day of slaughter. What I see here is that the lifestyle the rich had practiced for so long had become not just second nature but so addictive that he compared them to sheep or oxen, who, unaware of their approaching slaughter, continued to gorge themselves.[5]

While the fraudulent activities of the rich filled their coffers, the poor endured exploitation and deprivation. Yet it has not gone unnoticed. The day of reckoning and judgment for the rich will come.

James concludes the section by describing what the rich had done to the poor. Not only did they exploit the poor and condemn them to misery, they took them to the courts, in which one would have expected justice. However, their unfair practices extended there also. They used their wealth to control the judicial system and did not even bother to pretend to do justice. The next clause illustrates his meaning: "You have murdered the just" (verse 6). Some see here a reference to Jesus. I agree with Robertson that while there may be a resemblance to His trial and condemnation, there is probably no direct reference.[6]

Dikaios, when used with the neuter, can mean innocent.[7] Kittel admits this meaning of the term though he sees a moral implication as well.[8] Given this nuance, we can therefore see James as saying that the wealthy in their exploitation and control of the courts caused the death of innocent people. Moreover, even though *dikaios* is in the singular, it does not reference a single individual. It is the generic use of the singular with an inclusive article denoting class. The apostle has in mind a class of innocent people. He feels so strongly about this that he calls it murder. The rich have murdered innocent victims who do not even resist or oppose them. Doubtlessly, the latter were leaving it all in the hands of God, who said, "Vengeance is mine, I will repay."

Application

How does what James has to say apply to contemporary business relationships and wealthy individuals? Is it still relevant? My father told me the story of someone he knew who labored tirelessly to acquire wealth. A hard worker, he put long hours in his business and was not always kind and understanding toward his relatives or employees. At times he did not eat properly. His great life's goal was to be wealthy. He did well and soon got what he desired. Not only did he build a posh house—he purchased several others as well and three cars and a van. With his business thriving, he was on top of the world.

Unfortunately, however, before he had a chance to retire and begin to enjoy what he had accumulated, he became ill with several ailments attributable to the abuse he had heaped on his body in his drive for wealth. Whereas before he had spent health to get wealth, now he was spending wealth to regain health—but to no avail. It was too late. Like a dying Bob Marley, who whispered to his son Ziggy, "Money can't buy life," he discovered that money cannot purchase health or happiness as well as life. Contemporary Christians and others need to learn this lesson.

In the twenty-first-century corporate world it is a "dog-eat-dog situation." Ambition, exploitation, greed, self-centeredness, and avarice are among its attributes. Survival of the wittiest and the fearless, it is characterized by schmoozing, back-scratching, and networking. People climb over each other to reach the top. Some will do anything to climb the corporate ladder, but it can't be so with Christians. We have principles to maintain, a Savior to exemplify, a victory to win, a heaven to attain, and a hell to spurn. While others are exploiting their workers, we need to promote ours, and while others are duplicitous, we must seek justice, equality, fairness, integrity, fair play, truth, and right. We need to stand with and defend the defenseless. Having been freed by the Master for freedom, we cannot be part of any group or system that oppresses, enslaves, cheats, or berates anyone. Our responsibility is to be the conscience for workplaces, corporations, nations, and the world.

That means we'll not participate in unfair or unjust business practices. Some employers take the tax withholdings from their employees' wages but neither make those payments to the Internal Revenue Service and Social Security nor pay their own portion. But Christian employers can't follow their example. Other employers leave the money in the bank longer than necessary to get as much use of the funds as possible and thereby pay their employees in a less than timely manner. Christian employers can't do that, for Jesus would not. They will pay their employees on time and respect their obligations and those of their employees, remembering that Jesus asked us to deal with others as we would want them to treat us (Luke 6:31).

We could list still other practices that Christian entrepreneurs, managers, and other business professionals should avoid. While some companies take out their employees' health insurance contributions but do not actually pay the premiums or add their portion, Christian companies will not act in such a dishonest manner. Although some firms exploit undocumented workers—employing them when they shouldn't but paying them less than minimum wage and giving them less than ideal treatment because they cannot say anything for fear of being reported to the immigration services—Christian-owned or Christian-operated companies will respect the law and will treat others with fairness. Unlike some organizations that allow their workers' vacation time to accrue but won't allow them to take it as the law admonishes, Christian organizations will render to their workers the vacation time they have rightfully earned. And whereas some companies will not allow their employees to take the required lunch and other breaks given to those who work an eight-hour day, Christian companies will set the standard for justice, fair play, and honesty.

Likewise, while some people work and spend all they earn, Christians know that 10 percent of their earnings and another self-determined portion are not theirs but belong to God as tithes and offerings. They will not rob God but will return an honest tithe and a faithful offering. Furthermore, Christian-owned or Christian-operated institutions or businesses will not engage in deceptive advertising or other unconscionable acts. Nor will Christian entrepreneurs participate in pyramid schemes or knowingly sponsor a scam. Also, I believe that if James were here today he would speak out against the following business practices:

1. Cutting back on customer service levels to save money.
2. Replacing human beings with machines to answer our phones in order to increase the bottom line.

3.   Paying employees less to increase profits, since payroll is the single biggest expense line item.

4.   Not valuing family in the workplace.

5.   Discriminating against women by refusing to promote them too far up the ladder or by not giving them equal pay for equal work.

6.   Pretending to be equal-opportunity employers when they're not.

7.   Making business decisions during rough times at the expense of those who actually do the work.

8.   Surprising clients by adding unexpected expenses or hidden un-explained fees.

9.   Turning company and/or employee mistakes into client or con-sumer problems and/or expenses.

10.   Making misleading statements or unsubstantiated claims about a product or service.

11.   Price fixing—a number of businesses in an area agreeing to charge a certain price for a product regardless of the large markup involved.

12.   Predatory pricing—charging a price below production cost to kill small competitors.

Finally, modern rich people generally and Christians particularly need to learn the lessons James advocated. First, we cannot keep wealth under the belt. God gave it to us to share with others and to support causes that glorify Him. We need to exercise stewardship of the wallet and the purse. Regardless of their status in life, we will treat others with respect, fairness, justice, equality, and tolerance. Above all, we need to consecrate all that we possess as God directs, for not only is life uncertain, but wealth is fleeting and perishable. Only that used to enhance the kingdom of God and assist the needs of humanity will last.

---

[1] W. Barclay, *The Letters of James and Peter,* pp. 115, 116.

[2] *The SDA Bible Commentary,* vol. 7, p. 536.

[3] C. S. Keener, *IVP Bible Background Commentary,* p. 700.

[4] E. G. White, *The Desire of Ages,* pp. 100-102.

[5] A. T. Robertson, *Word Pictures,* vol. 6, p. 60.

[6] *Ibid.*

[7] William F. Arndt and F. Wilbur Gingrich, *A Greek-English Lexicon of the New Testament* (Chicago: University of Chicago Press, 1959), p. 195.

[8] Gerhard Kittel and Gerhard Friedrich, eds., *Theological Dictionary of the New Testament* (Grand Rapids: Wm. B. Eerdmans, 1964-1976), s.v. *dikaios.*

CHAPTER 11

Enduring Piety:
Its Joys and Sorrows

A story tells of a funeral convoy that entered a Scottish cemetery. It differed from others in that the chief mourner following the hearse was the dead man's dog—his closest survivor. After the service all the man's friends departed, but the dog would not leave his master's grave. Day after day for weeks people tried in vain to lure the dog away, but he would not leave the spot. Finally, they gave up and began feeding him there. There by his master's grave, for 14 years, the dog lived, until he died in 1872. A small monument acclaims the dog's faithfulness to the very end.

A similar story tells of a dog that followed its master's casket to a train station, where the animal stayed for several years, patiently awaiting his return. It died at the station. If dogs can be so faithful to earthly masters, why can't humans with their superior brains be loyal to their divine Master? Or is the superior brain the problem?

Enduring piety is necessary for salvation, but it has joys and sorrows. James begins, "Therefore be patient, brethren, until the coming of the Lord" (James 5:7). It marks a shift from censure of the rich to exhortation of the saints. Returning to the word *adelphos* ("brothers"), he begins with a call to patience. It has an ambiguity or perhaps duality about it. While some commentators pick up on the theme of the Second Advent, and rightly so, something else motivated it. Walvoord and Zuck are correct in seeing a transition here when they say, "From the rich, James turned to the restless. For these he again used the friendly address, 'brothers.' The tone turns from stark condemnation to sensitive consolation. James excoriated the rich but encouraged the receptive."[1]

While what they say is true, we must not overlook a three-letter Greek word that makes a big difference here. James says, "Be patient therefore" (KJV). The "therefore" refers back to the prior verses. The rich are prospering despite their unjust behaviors, unholy actions, and murderous practices. But verse 7 predicts their impending judgment. Christians should thus be patient, for the reign of terror by the rich and their instigator—the devil—might be long but won't be forever. The wicked shall *not* rule forever over God's people. Their demise is coming. In the meantime, however, we need patience.

While we have already defined patience,[2] James uses a different word, *makrothymēsate,* here. It comes from "a compound of 'long' (*makros*) and 'temper' (*thymos*). The idea is to set the timer of one's temper for a long run. Think long [before responding]. Focus on the final lap in the race of life."[3] Why this kind of patience? First, because while the rich flourish now, they are only preparing their hearts for their day of reckoning—the coming of the Lord—that is on its way. We can afford to wait because God will assuredly take care of the situation.

Second, such a call for patience implies that Christ's return may involve a delay. Patience is endurance under delay, suffering, or trials. The idea that there is a delay we find reinforced by the adverbial preposition *heōs,* which denotes the end of a time period. James was summoning his readers to unwearyingly endure whatever transpired from then until the Second Advent. It is also a call to let the anticipated joys, pleasures, and happiness associated with the Advent be a source of motivation until its arrival. It is even evident from this statement that James and his readers may have anticipated Christ's return in their day.

James's exhortation responds to an implied question he knows may have plagued his readers. Given all the injustices of the rich, it asks, why are they still prospering and for how long will they continue to dominate God's people? The question was not new, but that fact did not make it any less troubling for James. David had grappled with it, as we see in Psalm 73:2, 3: "But as for me, my feet had almost stumbled; my steps had nearly slipped. For I was envious of the boastful, when I saw the prosperity of the wicked." Habakkuk confronted God with it in Habakkuk 1:1-4 and 1:12-2:1.

"You are of purer eyes than to behold evil,
    And cannot look on wickedness.
    Why do You look on those who deal treacherously,
    And hold Your tongue when the wicked devours
    A person more righteous than he? . . .
    Shall they therefore empty their net,

And continue to slay nations without pity?
I will stand my watch
And set myself on the rampart,
And watch to see what He will say to me" (Hab. 1:13-2:1).

Many of us may still be grappling with the issue. We too need to take heart, learn from James's response and other scriptural teachings, and continue to set our timers and focus on the Second Advent. It is much nearer now than then. The apostle here asks believers to look beyond the problems and difficulties of the present to the goal ahead. They need to set their gazes on it, get their motivation from it, and let it brighten any dark spots in their life. Scripture does not call it the blessed hope for nothing. Let's use it as insulation, inspiration, anticipation, and illumination. To assist believers in getting his point, James employs another illustration from nature and agriculture. "See how the farmer waits for the precious fruit of the earth, waiting patiently for it until it receives the early and latter rain" (James 5:7).

Because biblical society was agrarian, much of Scripture's imagery reflects that setting. Here James uses a picture of farmers who, after planting seeds, must wait for the harvest, since nothing they do can control the process. My major professor, himself from Jerusalem, used to say, "Geography influences theology." This is precisely what we see here. Palestine is very dry and arid between June and September. The autumn rains (early) of mid-October to November soften and water the ground to allow the farmer to plow and plant seeds. The December/January rainfall penetrates the soil deeply, thus allowing the crops to grow. Without this rain, the seeds would not germinate. The spring rains (latter) coming in March/April promoted the maturing and ripening of the grain for harvest. Otherwise there would be no ready grain—precious fruit of the earth—to harvest.[4]

James employed this geographical/agricultural phenomenon as a spiritual and theological illustration, just as the Old Testament prophets had done. Jesus sowed the seeds. The outpouring of the early rain at Pentecost prepared the soil and germinated the seeds. We await the latter rain to ripen and mature the crop. Just as the farmer needs patience to wait for nature to do its work to assure a good harvest, so Christians must allow Christ's agent—the Holy Spirit—time to attain a good work in and through us. James says, "You also be patient." If farmers willingly exercise patience to go through the agricultural cycle to receive a good harvest, Christians must be willing to endure the needed hardships to produce a good spiritual harvest. We must let the Lord do His work in and through us to have a mature harvest for the Lord's return.

Significantly, James makes no reference to the early rain, perhaps because he knew it had already occurred at Pentecost. Now what was necessary was to let the latter rain develop the harvest. Therefore, he again exhorts the saints to patience, adding, "Establish your hearts, for the coming of the Lord is at hand" (verse 8). The coming of the Lord—the harvest—requires the latter rain for the maturing and ripening of precious fruit—the souls for whom Christ died. That is why we must unceasingly pray for the Spirit's outpouring as we prepare ourselves to receive it. I believe here is one way to establish our hearts for the Lord's return. Barclay calls it the confirming of our faith,[5] and certainly today's stressful time requires it.

One of the foibles of human nature is the inclination to turn on each other during difficult times. To deter Christians, called "brethren" here, from such an all too common tendency, James says, "Do not grumble against one another, brethren, lest you be condemned" (verse 9). The command is stronger in Greek than the translation allows. Use of the present imperative with *mē* signals the cessation of an action already in progress. Thus the directive is to stop grumbling or murmuring against one another. The passage means that they were actually doing it, and James wanted it to end. It was what Israel had done against each other and against God on the borders of Canaan.

James states an unwanted outcome of that action—they will be condemned. Perhaps he was alluding to some of the issues already presented in James 4. They should not be allowed to create separations or discord. It was too near the end, for already he says, "The Judge is standing at the door" (James 5:9). Jesus, James declares, is standing at the door, prepared to take action. It speaks to the immediacy of the Second Advent.[6] Such imminence demands readiness to meet Him, which implies that we must be ready, not just getting ready. Because we don't know when our Lord returns, we must always be prepared. So it was not a time for being involved with petty grievances or mission-distracting accusations and fights. Now was the time for concentrated focus on the Advent.

Yet, how do we relate to James saying Jesus was then standing at the door ready to come and now 2,000 years later He still hasn't returned? How do we sustain hope under such strain? It is a significant issue. As previously stated, James and many of his contemporaries thought they would see the Advent in their lifetime. Many in past generations felt that way too, and others in our age believe they will see Jesus' appearing. We must recall that Jesus never gave a date for His return. Those who in anticipation set a time are only expressing their own desires. We should not let their feelings or opinions discourage or get us off track. Jesus said no one but the Father knows the time of His return. Peter declared that the Advent's supposed delay is providential, since "the Lord is not slack concerning His promise, as some count slackness, but is longsuffering toward us, not willing that any should perish but that all should come to repentance" (2 Peter 3:9). Most interesting is the fact that even if Christ does not return to the world tomorrow, we can die at any time, and that to us would be His coming. Everyone must be ready for such an eventuality. It is something that we must take seriously. Preparing for it should take priority over any focus on a supposed delay, because it involves our eternal salvation. Thus we can't afford to treat it lightly.

To ensure that he reached the hearts of his readers with his urgent and vital appeal, James went from "brethren" (*adelphos*, James 5:9) to "my brethren" (*adelphos mou*, verse 10). It continues his trend of winning address. To further reinforce the need for patience, he cites the prophets who spoke in the name of the Lord as an example of suffering and patience. One would have thought that speaking for God would have granted them respect and shielded them from hostility, but sadly it did not make them immune from the ire of people, even kings. Some were mistreated and others executed, but all faced intense opposition. Their perseverance and steadfast courage despite the odds can serve to uplift those who are discouraged.

Verse 11 continues in the same vein, but its opening line presents a universal truth. James says, as you know, that we consider blessed those who endure. Some scholars see an allusion here to 4 Maccabees. Others sense a hint to the Beatitudes, and still others Matthew 24:13. In reference to the first view, Moo observes:

"At the opening of his book, after introducing Eleazar, his seven brothers, and their mother as his model martyrs, the author of 4 Maccabees says, 'It is fitting for me to praise for their virtues those who, with their mother, died for the sake of nobility and goodness, but I would call them blessed for the honor in which they are held' (1:10). So James shows his dependence on this tradition once more in his opening words in this verse: *As you know, we consider blessed those who have persevered.*"[7]

Located in 2 Maccabees 7, the story tells of a mother and seven sons killed by Antiochus Epiphanes. Just before the Maccabean revolt started, the Syrians captured and ordered them to eat pork. When the first brother refused, the soldiers heated huge pans red-hot, dismembered him, and roasted him alive before his mother and brothers, who encouraged him to endure courageously. Each brother had the same fate; then their mother also died. Fourth Maccabees and other Jewish works retell the story to rally the faithful to steadfastness.

Yet given the many times James refers to the teaching of Jesus, especially the Sermon on the Mount, in his brief pamphlet, it would not be surprising that he alludes to it here. Matthew 5:12 explicitly says, "Rejoice and be exceedingly glad, for great is your reward in heaven, for so they persecuted the prophets who were before you." The reference to the persecution of the prophets in James 5:10 and his citing of them as an example of suffering and patience are not coincidental. It is indeed possible that he sees this beatitude as saying that those who endure are blessed. In fact, it may have become the view of the church and so his "we count them blessed who endure" (verse 11) would have been not only understood but was a shared sentiment.

It is feasible that Matthew 24:13 ("But he who endures to the end shall be saved") may also have influenced him. While it does not specifically mention being blessed, the final outcome of endurance—salvation—can be seen as and may indeed have been viewed as such by the early church. Again, these are the specific words of Jesus and would have been treasured. Thus it is easy to see how the tradition as described here could have emerged around them. The point is that James and his contemporaries regarded those who endured and withstood suffering as blessed. It is also not impossible that all three sources may have inspired the statement, but there is yet a fourth influence, and it is not conjectural.

In James 5:11 he says, "You have heard of the perseverance of Job and seen the end intended by the Lord—that the Lord is very compassionate and merciful." Where did they hear it? It seems he has the synagogue in mind, remembering that he is speaking to the 12 tribes in the Diaspora. While it's true Job did not display the kind of patience James has described thus far, he did survive the test without renouncing his faith in God. Although Job questioned God, he did withstand the temptation to curse Him and die; and though he justified himself to his friends, he did face the accusations of alleged friends who questioned his integrity and charged him with secret sins when he knew he hadn't done anything wrong. How many of us could have endured that along with the loss of all our children and our possessions while still maintaining our integrity?

James legitimately used Job as an example here. Yet note that he does not employ him as an example of patience or endurance. Rather, he speaks of his perseverance. What is the difference? The first, *hupomonē*, as seen before, refers to remaining or abiding under something for a long time and therefore requires fortitude. It is not passive but describes "that gallant spirit which can breast the tides of doubt and sorrow and disaster and come out with faith still stronger on the other side."[8] The second word, *makrothumia*, implies restraint, not losing heart, forbearing, or steadfastness. James used the former here to describe Job. The patriarch did remain under the trials and pressures of the devil for a long period while not knowing what was going on.

Despite what some may think about the aptness of James's use of Job as an example, we must not forget that God had assurance in Job's ability to endure the trials and suffering that Satan sent. He confidently dared Satan to consider His servant Job's ability to withstand it. The Lord even removed His protective shield from around the man. That is a lot of confidence in a human being. Could it be that our problems, trials, and temptations are expressions of God's confidence in us and our ability to endure? When we gripe, complain, and lose heart in suffering, are we saying to God that He has misplaced His trust in us? We need to work with Him as He does with us. He will see us through.

James asked the "brethren" to look at the final outcome God intended for Job. Robertson renders the phrase as "the conclusion wrought by the Lord."[9] The two goals listed are compassion and mercy. If some of James's readers had problems with why they were having difficulties while being faithful to God, Job's experience could serve to allay their fears. They could have confidence in God's largeheartedness and mercy. Not only would God not allow them to encounter more than they could bear, but ultimately the testing of their faith would bring good results. Job's experience says we can trust God and His purposes for us and allow trials to have their designed end—building patient endurance.

The next verse is somewhat problematic in that scholars are unsure where it belongs. Some see it as not connecting with either what precedes or what follows it. "But above all, my brethren, do not swear, either by heaven or by earth or with any other oath. But let your 'Yes' be 'Yes,' and your 'No,' 'No,' lest you fall into judgment" (verse 12). While the prior verses deal with patience and the succeeding ones with prayer, we must not forget that the original manuscripts had no punctuation marks to separate thoughts. That said, we must also note that the section begins with a command not to grumble against each other. A climax that calls for Christians to be circumspect in their speech is not only fitting but poignant. What does James mean by this?

He seems to have been motivated by the words of Jesus as seen in Matthew 5:33-37. Swearing here does not refer to the use of expletives or four-letter words but a prohibition against oaths. James calls us to take what we say seriously, an appeal for our words to be "sound" or "unimpaired."[10] Above all, it is a summons to integrity. And what is integrity? It's "the state of being whole, entire, or undiminished."[11] When we have integrity, it means that we keep our promises and do what we say we will do by when we say we will do it. And if for any reason we fail to fulfill our word, our promises, we set things right immediately by apologizing or stating that we will be unable to follow through.

Being true to our words sets us apart from ordinary people who don't treasure theirs, or think little of them. It is our ability to honor our promises that others use to decide if we are trustworthy. We must remember that our word is our bond. That is what Jesus meant and what James wanted us to understand. Those who have integrity will not need to use heaven, earth, or God to substantiate the veracity of their statements. Their words will be whole and sound and thus won't condemn them.

Application

Some time ago I met a young man who gave up belief in God and left the church. Desiring to know what caused the change, I asked what I could do to assist in rekindling his faith. "My parents told me," he said, "that their parents told them that their parents told them that their parents told them that Jesus was coming soon. He has not yet come and there is no evidence that He is going to arrive any time soon. I am tired of the wait, so I have given up all hope of a soon-returning Savior." How tragic!

His experience demonstrates that the message of James is just as applicable today as when first given 2,000 years ago. People in our postmodern age need patience to hold on to their faith. We find at least three things highlighted in the passage we have examined: (1) an undercurrent of murmuring by the saints; (2) the impatience of the saints; and (3) the tendency of Christians to focus on time and the delay of the Advent. Israel murmured against Moses and God in the wilderness on the very borders of the Promised Land. That postponed their entry, as the Lord made them spend 40 years during which that generation died and so did not enter Canaan. We are on the borders of the heavenly Canaan. As Hebrews 3 and 4 admonish, we need to learn from their experience. Instead of murmuring and judging each other, we must focus on what matters most. God has neither designated us as people gazers or sin police nor placed us in charge of the salvation of anyone else but ourselves. W. H. Bellamy said more than 100 years ago, "O wait! Meekly wait and murmur not." Therefore, since the Judge is standing at the door, let's do the assigned task and leave the rest to Him.

The saints can be very impatient. We need things done yesterday. So the Second Coming must be now. Yet we are not in charge. God is. Salvation belongs to the Lord—not to us. As the recipients and the objects of God's grace, we can't and must not dictate the terms or time of salvation. That is divine prerogative! Our task is to be ready for the Advent and help others to prepare for it. Harold Camping was one of the latest to learn that God, not humanity, is in control. All his predictions about the date of the Advent failed. We must learn from what Moses told Israel long ago: "Do not be afraid. Stand still, and see the salvation of the Lord" (Ex. 14:13). James adds: "You too, be patient and stand firm, because the Lord's coming is near" (James 5:8, NIV). God is full of compassion and mercy, but they won't last forever nor should they be slighted.

While clearly we are tired of the present world and long for heaven, too many saints focus on the wrong thing—delay and passing time. God designated us neither "Advent watchers" nor "Time police." Our task is to make disciples and accomplish His mission. A focus on time or delay leads to doubt, discouragement, frustration, and a desire to quit. Now more than ever before we must remember that while we revel in time, God dwells in eternity, and what seems like an eternity to us is but a moment to Him. The present is only an interlude designed for our reclamation. Let's live in it, maximize it, and use it for God's glory.

Therefore, I would caution us against thinking about a delay, for how can there be a delay when we did not have an arrival time in the first place? Also, I would suggest that we use the time spent in murmuring about a delay instead preparing for the day of the Lord that will come. And, if not to the whole world tomorrow, it could arrive to you or me in death. Moreover, let us remember Peter's suggestion that what seems like a delay to us is a matter of the Lord's providential patience (2 Peter 3:9).

May I therefore invite us to think positively, exercise patience, stand firm in the faith, learn from the positive examples of people of faith, saturate ourselves in the Word, maintain an atmosphere of prayer at all times, and never pass over an opportunity to share the goodness and mercies of God with another. If we do these things, the God of grace will endow us with patience and faith to endure to the end.

---

[1] John F. Walvoord and Roy B. Zuck, *The Bible Knowledge Commentary: An Exposition of the Scriptures* (Wheaton, Ill.: Victor Books, 1985), vol. 2, p. 833.

[2] For a discussion of patience, see pp. 26, 27.

[3] Walvoord and Zuck.

[4] See *SDA Bible Dictionary,* pp. 830, 831; W. Barclay, *The Letters of James and Peter,* p. 121; C. S. Keener, *The IVP Bible Background Commentary,* p. 702.

[5] Barclay, *The Letters of James and Peter,* p. 121.

[6] *The SDA Bible Commentary,* vol. 7, p. 539.

[7] D. J. Moo, *The Letter of James,* p. 227.

[8] Barclay, *The Letters of James and Peter,* p. 125.

[9] A. T. Robertson, *Word Pictures,* vol. 6, p. 62.

[10] www.dictionary.com, s.v. "integrity."

[11] *Ibid.*

CHAPTER 12

The Efficacy of Prayer

Archimedes said that if he had a place to stand on and a lever long enough, he could lift the world. Although he never found either one, "we have something to stand upon—the immutable word of God. We have a lever on earth—the power of prayer. With prayer planted on the Word of God we can lift the world heavenward, even up to the throne on high. Intercessors, girdle the world with your prayers! They have a power unequaled by any material agency."[1] Tennyson was more correct than he himself knew when he placed the following words in King Arthur's mouth for Sir Bedivere as he entered the barge to depart: "Pray for my soul. More things are wrought by prayer than this world dreams of. Wherefore, let thy voice rise like a fountain for me night and day."[2]

What is prayer? Although variously defined, it is seen as communication with God, and indeed it is. Of the nine definitions that Webster[3] lists, the following are especially germane:

1. A devout petition to God or an object of faith.
2. A spiritual communion with God or an object of worship, as in supplication, thanksgiving, adoration, or confession.
3. The act or practice of praying to God or an object of worship.
4. A petition or entreaty.

James Montgomery's definition says that prayer is "the soul's sincere desire, uttered or unexpressed . . . the simplest form of speech . . . the contrite sinner's voice . . . the Christian's vital breath . . . [and] native air."[4] Ellen White viewed it as "the opening of the heart to God as to a friend."[5] Again: "Prayer is the key in the hand of faith to unlock heaven's storehouse, where are treasured the boundless resources of Omnipotence."[6] Thus she advises Christians to begin their day with prayer,[7] since prayer is as essential as daily food,[8] since it nourishes[9] and is vital to the religious life and experience.[10] Mohandas Gandhi said of prayer that "properly understood and applied, it is the most potent instrument of action."[11] The Jewish philosopher Martin Buber adds: "In prayer man pours himself out, dependent without reservation, knowing that, incomprehensibly, he acts on God, albeit without exacting anything from God."[12]

In the amazing discipline of prayer we have the most potent yet most underestimated, neglected, and unappreciated force in the world. Why the paradox? I believe that some don't understand it, others can't be bothered to take the time to learn it, and still others give up, since it seems that their prayers never get answered. Some, assuming that God doesn't even exist, ask to whom do we pray? If God is nothing more than a human creation, do we pray to ourselves?

On the other hand, we have many others enthralled by the ritual of prayer. They believe in it, practice it numerous times daily, and praise God continuously for the answers to their prayers. They cling to faith and are sure God is real, since they see interventions on their behalf. How do we explain such extreme reactions? What is the function of prayer in the life of a Christian disciple? It is to this subject that James now turns.

He begins with the matter of affliction or suffering. The "among you" in James 5:13 says he is speaking to members of the community. He assumes that they are not immune to tragedy. In fact, he had invited them in James 1:2 to count it joy when they faced trials and difficulties. His optimistic outlook and inspiring recommendation notwithstanding, suffering and ailment tend to lead to sadness and gloom. Although it is impossible to live the Christian life without having some kind of suffering, many people wilt under its strain, while others complain or struggle with depression. While many do respond in such ways, it does not have to be that way.

James offers a better one, especially for a Christian. "Let him pray" (James 5:13), he urges. Since it is the present imperative in Greek, it is a call to continue an action already in progress. Even if an answer is not immediately forthcoming, we should not despair or give up but continue to pray. The bottom line is that times of affliction should send us to our knees in prayer to God, not push us to our toes in flight from Him. Times of infirmity and weakness are prayer opportunities. Prayer changes things, so pray not just when you feel like it but even when you don't. Make it a habit. It is a good one to have.

The second half of the verse shifts to the opposite emotion: "Is anyone cheerful or joyful?" James asks. It is a feeling that some do not associate with the Christian life. Some Christians think that the longer the face, the greater the piety. A story tells of a father who took his son for an afternoon walk in the park. As they strolled along, the boy shouted, "Daddy, Daddy, look! I see a Christian over there." Puzzled, the father saw no sign of another person nearby. Yet his son insisted, "Daddy, Daddy, I see a Christian over there."

With some frustration, he followed the gaze and pointing finger of his son. What he saw shocked and amazed him. He reflected on what they must have taught for his son to arrive at such a conclusion. To his amazement he realized that his son was pointing at a donkey. For, if by definition a Christian is a person with a long face, few other candidates, if any, can rival a donkey. Let us not misrepresent the Christian life but demonstrate that every day with Jesus is sweeter than the one before. The best way to do so is to learn to praise. It is what James advises. "Let him pray. Is anyone cheerful? Let him sing psalms" (verse 13). The Greek word translated "singing psalms" actually means "singing praise." Praise is not a bad word or an evil practice. Even Jesus, God's Son, does praise according to Hebrews 2:12. If He praises God, we also must to do the same. Christians need to practice praise.

The psalmist says, "Praise the Lord! Praise the Lord, O my soul! I will praise the Lord as long as I live; I will sing praises to my God all my life long" (Ps. 146:1, 2, NRSV). Again: "Praise the Lord! How good it is to sing praises to our God; for he is gracious, and a song of praise is fitting" (Ps. 147:1, NRSV). Nothing can change one's mood from gloom to gladness better than praise. And a very effective form of praise is singing, as the psalmist declares. It was Jesus Himself who "filled the earth with beauty, and the air with song."[13] Praising Him in song for the beauty of the earth and blessings of life is bound to benefit Christians. It was one thing that sustained Jesus while He lived among us.

"Jesus carried into His labor cheerfulness and tact. It requires much patience and spirituality to bring Bible religion into the home life and into the workshop, to bear the strain of worldly business, and yet keep the eye single to the glory of God. This is where Christ was a helper. He was never so full of worldly care as to have no time or thought for heavenly things. Often He expressed the gladness of His heart *by singing psalms and heavenly songs. Often the dwellers in Nazareth heard His voice raised in praise and thanksgiving to God. He held communion with heaven in song.*"[14]

I have found a highly effective recipe for discouragement and depression very similar to what Jesus did. Throughout my years in ministry I have recommended it to parishioners and students who have found it helpful. I invite them at such times to think about and write down as many blessings as they can recall that the Lord has recently given them. Then they should praise Him for each one. People have reported that as they begin to write down the blessings their mood starts to change, and by the time they arrive at praising God for their blessings they find themselves in a better attitude. It works! Why not try it on and see if it fits you? I guarantee that you will be happy you did! It is what Jesus did to assist others: "As His companions complained of weariness from labor, they were cheered by the sweet melody from His lips. His praise seemed to banish the evil angels, and, like incense, fill the place with fragrance."[15] That is what praise does. Let us praise the Lord!

We move next to a subject that not only everyone in James's community but everyone everywhere can identify with—sickness. That the apostle again has the community of faith in mind we find indicated by the phrase "among you" (James 5:14). Sickness here does not seem to be slight ailments or minor sniffles. The apostle employs the present tense of a verb implying "to be weak or without strength." It seems to refer to someone weakened by a debilitating disease or who has a prolonged strength-sapping bout with some malady. The tendency is to leave such situations to the physician. James outlines a plan for such Christians to follow that would highlight the fact that God Himself delights in taking care of such issues.

James says such individuals should call for the elders of the church. It is significant that the request should not come from relatives of the sick, fellow members, or even the elders of the church themselves. The instructions are explicit and unmistakable. "Let him call" refers back to "is anyone among you sick?" Those who are sick must make the petition. It is their faith that is first required, and then that of the elders. While relatives, friends, and fellow members can be supportive, the sick individual must initiate the call.

James also has explicit instructions for the elders. They are to pray over the sick and anoint them with oil in the name of the Lord. Anointing must accompany the special prayer. The Jews had used anointing in two ways: (1) ordinary anointing to facilitate personal cleansing and (2) official anointing to consecrate kings, priests, and prophets.[16] Christians employed it in conjunction with prayer for healing. Was James aware that when Jesus sent the Twelve out on their first mission trip they had anointed the sick with oil and had healed many? It appears that he was and that he may have based his instructions on this tradition, but one cannot rule out the cleansing implication. Moreover, he may have been present when Jesus told the story of the good Samaritan who used oil for medicinal purposes. At any rate, Robertson makes a fascinating observation: "The use of olive oil was one of the best remedial agencies known to the ancients. They used it internally and externally."[17] Clearly, here was a summons to engage in divine healing for the sick person accompanied by use of a remedial agency known for its medicinal value.

Doubtless, though, the emphasis here is on the value of the prayer and the faith of both the ill individual and the one praying the prayer, as is made clear by the fact that both the prayer and the anointing should be done in the Lord's name. Elders are human instruments through whom the Lord works but God is the true source. It should give us pause when we see people going around claiming powers of healing, calling attention to themselves and distributing business cards labeling themselves as professional faith healers. Such people promote themselves, not God or His cause. Gifts from God should make us humble and dependent on Him. The glory for such achievements should go to Him and not to the human agency. It is how we can differentiate those working for God and those relying on and promoting self.

Some modern Christians, however, do not take their prescribed medicines but want to rely solely on prayer—not the prayer of healing just mentioned, but regular prayer. Years ago I met a member at a church in another country whose blood pressure was an outrageous 220/110 and who was obviously not taking his medication. I encouraged him to go to the doctor and to use his prescriptions. But he got upset and charged me with undermining his faith. Is this faith or presumption? Clearly James was recommending prayer by the elders along with use of a recognized medicinal agent. Some modern doctors still use it.

We must not overlook or slight this combination of medicine and divine intervention. Could it be that anointing with oil also served to calm the nerves, sending stimulation to the brain that, coupled with faith, served to trigger the process of healing? God uses physicians to effect not only physical healing but, where they are cooperative, spiritual healing, too. I am blessed with an ophthalmologist who prays for me on each visit as well as before and during procedures in the operating room. Actually, both his office and the operating room are saturated with songs of praise. God bless Dr. Ronald Anderson! It is also my conviction that people should not make it a case of either prayer or medication. It should be both, especially if one has a physician who combines natural and traditional medicine, as Dr. Theodore Watkins does.

Verse 15 concurs with the notion that the emphasis is on the value of prayer. "The prayer of faith will save the sick, and the Lord will raise him up. And if he has committed sins, he will be forgiven." Not only does it speak to the potency of prayer, but it sets the condition for answered prayer. It is the prayer of faith that will save the sick. But it is not the prayer, even of faith, that will effect the healing. It is the Lord Himself. The prayer of faith is the human way of reaching out to the Lord and relying on His omnipotent and omniscient wisdom and providence to grant requests. While it's true that faith is "the substance of things hoped for, the evidence of things not seen" (Heb. 11:1), it is more than that. It involves turning over all our affairs and life to God, depending on Him completely, trusting Him implicitly, following Him unconditionally, and putting our confidence in Him absolutely. Such faith gets rewarded.

But we find still more blessings to gain. *Sōzō*, translated "save," is fascinating. While its basic meaning is "to save," it also has the connotation of healing. What we find here then is that the prayer of faith will heal the sick, but it also has a saving or a spiritual dimension. Thus we see that not only will the sick person be restored, but if they have committed sins, they will also receive forgiveness. Some limit the forgiveness here to sins that may relate to the condition being healed, but while that is a possible implication it is not the only one. We find precedents for such situations in the ministry of Jesus. He not only attended to people's need for physical healing, but He forgave their sins and restored them to new life (see Matt. 9:1-8; Mark 5:1-18; and Luke 5:17-26).

As a student in college, I experienced eight Weeks of Prayer (Weeks of Spiritual Emphasis) and in graduate school I went through several more. One observation that stands out from them is that some people do not comprehend the biblical teaching of confession. I have heard individuals publicly relate matters that occurred privately and that should have remained that way. Such confessions often came back to haunt them. Is that what James meant? I think not! How then should we interpret "confess your sins to one another"? Robertson says, "Confession of sin to God is already assumed. But public confession of certain sins to one another in the meetings is greatly helpful in many ways."[18]

The Greek actually has "therefore" at the beginning of James 5:16, which suggests it is a follow-up of the argument already set forth. It means it is related to the issue of praying for the sick and forgiveness of sins. The implication is that confession of sins to God should precede the prayer for the sick, thus allowing nothing to block the way. In other words, James reminds the saints that there needs to be confession of sins to one another where applicable. "The prime requirement for sincere faith in prayer is a clear conscience. Wrong deeds secretly done are to be confessed to God alone. Sins that involve others are to be confessed also to those who have suffered injury."[19]

That this is the proper context we find verified by the rest of the verse. James says that prayer for each other should follow confession of sins and the purpose is healing. Through such prayer and confession the sick, and those interceding on their behalf, will clear the way and ensure that nothing blocks the divine granting of their request. We should not forget that after the initial defeat at Ai, Joshua went to pray, but God told him to get up and first remove the "accursed thing" before praying. While the contexts are different, the principle is the same. God will not hear us if we cling to iniquity in our hearts and if the way is not clear to allow free access of His grace and power. The sick will ensure they have made all things right with God and fellow human beings, while the intercessors will remove any unresolved issue that could prevent the answering of the prayer and the healing of the sick.

It is interesting that verse 16 has two references to prayer. The first is a call to pray for one another. In our grief-filled and troubled world we need each other and each other's prayer more than many are willing to admit. Many who try to act big and independent are just trying to hide the pain and dependence that they feel. Let us neither neglect nor ignore James's summons.

The second reference is puzzling for scholars who are not sure if it should go with what precedes it or what follows. More important for us is the message that it holds: "The prayer of a good person has a powerful effect" (verse 16, TEV). We should pray for each other generally and each other's healing particularly—when requested—for a good person's prayer is potent. As for me, it is an awesome climax to the foregoing section while at the same time serving as a fitting introduction to what follows. Elijah is a fitting example of a good person whose fervent prayer had a powerful effect.

James says that the prophet "was a human being, even as we are. He prayed earnestly that it would not rain, and it did not rain on the land for three and a half years" (verse 17, NIV). As one of us, he was tempted as we are but remained steadfast. Although zealous for God and for right he still had his own foibles, as does each one of us. Yet in prayer he knew his utter dependence on the omnipotent arm and relied on His awesome grace. Elijah prayed for it not to rain. God heard and answered, and it did not rain for three and a half years. Interestingly, the famine would have affected him and indeed did, yet he did not question God. He carried out the instructions the Lord gave him and relied on God to provide for his needs. It is a great example of the kind of wholehearted dependence and unquestioning obedience to God that Christians ought to have. We certainly need such faith in today's world.

At the end of the stated three and a half years Elijah again prayed to God. This time he prayed for the drought to cease and for the rain to return. God heard and answered his prayer. Rain resumed once more, and the earth started to yield its crops. What James wanted his readers to understand is that Elijah was not a superhuman person. He was one of us, and if his prayers were powerful, so can be those of any Christian who obediently depends on God.

I can hear someone asking, If the prayer of faith by a good individual has a powerful impact, why aren't we seeing more miracles today? Why aren't our prayers as effective? These questions deserve good answers. The best I can give comes from two statements of Jesus. The first, "According to your faith let it be to you" (Matt. 9:29), suggests that if they are not, then it is because we are not exercising the necessary faith required.

The second is, "Most assuredly, I say to you, he who believes in Me, the works that I do he will do also; and greater works than these he will do, because I go to My Father. And whatever you ask in My name, that I will do, that the Father may be glorified in the Son. If you ask anything in My name, I will do it" (John 14:12-14). There is no limit here on what Jesus will do. So again, if we are not seeing the kind of miraculous answers to prayer that we would expect, the reason could be that we are not asking as we should. Maybe some prayers are halfhearted or uttered in doubting, or some of us are not claiming God's promises as we should. In addition, we must remember that while we make the requests, God does the answering, and He is the one who chooses the response.

We must also not forget that there are four possible answers to prayer:

yes, no, wait, and I have something better for you. While we need to ensure we do our part in terms of faith and readiness, we still have to leave the rest to God, keeping in mind that He did not answer Paul's prayer for healing. The apostle had a thorn in the flesh—a messenger of Satan to buffet him. He pleaded with the Lord on three occasions to remove it. Yet God did not answer those prayers affirmatively. Instead, He told Paul that His grace was sufficient to keep him (2 Cor. 12:7-9). Whatever the case, let's trust His providence!

Application

Do we still need prayer in the postmodern twenty-first century? Isn't it an obsolete practice from some bygone millennia? Let me share a story. An African missionary would travel overnight on a bicycle each Thursday to get remittances to the bank early on Friday mornings. He had a favorite spot where he slept each Thursday evening. Some youth from the village learned of his usual routine.

One Thursday they followed him, intending to steal all the cash he carried. Reaching his overnight spot, he settled in for the night. But as they prepared to attack, to their surprise they saw 27 armed men guarding him. They could not get close to him at all. The next morning the missionary got up and left. When they saw him a few days later, they asked him about the men who had been with him that night. Puzzled, he told them that he had been alone, as always. Explaining that they had attempted to rob him, they insisted that they had seen 27 men guarding him. The missionary was amazed, because he knew he had been alone.

Later that year he returned home on furlough. At his home church he related the story of his protection that night. An elder asked if he recalled the exact date of the experience. When the missionary shared it, the elder told of being awakened that morning with an intense desire to pray for him, because he sensed the missionary was in danger. He called 26 other men who joined him in prayer. Is prayer still effective? Twenty-seven individuals prayed for the missionary, and the would-be robbers saw 27 guards surrounding him. The angels of the Lord answered those prayers. We must heed the leading of the Spirit and pray for others when prompted by God. Although we might not know what they are experiencing and why the Lord wants us to pray, we must obediently commit to becoming prayer warriors. God needs more of them.

If ever a generation needed to spend more time on its knees, it is the present one. In a time when so many are dying from cancer, heart disease, hypertension, and HIV/AIDS, we must earnestly pray the prayer of faith for the sick. Cancer has become a leading killer. It strikes so many people today, leaving spouses and infant children. Does God care and can He cure cancer? See the appendix for a fairly modern deliverance resulting from prayers of faith for healing. God is the same yesterday, today, and forevermore. What He has done in the past He can do again. Let's trust His leading. We need more prayer warriors and intercessors. Will you commit to that task for the Lord?

----

[1] A. Nasby, *Treasury of the Christian World,* p. 261.

[2] *The Passing of Arthur,* cited in *The Oxford Dictionary of Quotations,* 3rd ed. (Oxford, Eng.: Oxford University Press, 1980), p. 535.

[3] *Webster's New Universal Unabridged Dictionary* (New York: Barnes and Noble, 2003), s.v. "prayer."

[4] Written in 1818 at the request of Edward Bickersteth for his book *Treatise on Prayer.*

[5] E. G. White, *Steps to Christ,* p. 93.

[6] *Ibid.,* p. 94.

[7] E. G. White, *Testimonies,* vol. 4, p. 588.

[8] Ellen G. White, *Messages to Young People* (Washington, D.C.: Review and Herald Pub. Assn., 1930), p. 114.

[9] E. G. White, *Testimonies,* vol. 4, p. 535.

[10] E. G. White, *Messages to Young People,* p. 182.

[11] Mohandas K. Gandhi, cited in Gerald Tomlinson, *Treasury of Religious Quotations* (Eaglewood Cliffs, N.J.: Prentice Hall, 1991), p. 187.

[12] Martin Buber, cited in *Treasury of Religious Quotations,* p. 187.

[13] E. G. White, *The Desire of the Ages,* p. 20.

[14] *Ibid.,* p. 73. (Italics supplied.)

[15] *Ibid.*

[16] *SDA Bible Dictionary,* p. 48.

[17] A. T. Robertson, *Word Pictures,* vol. 6, p. 64.

[18] *Ibid.,* p. 65.

[19] *The SDA Bible Commentary,* vol. 7, p. 541.

CHAPTER 13

Reclaiming the Lost

One of the major challenges of the Christian church has to do with how we respond to lost and/or missing members. Unfortunately it has not always shown that it knows how to deal redemptively with its own. It has been said that many places have more former Christians than those attending church. We do have a responsibility for them. What should be our approach and how do we discharge our responsibility? James 5:19, 20 declares, "Brethren, if anyone among you wanders from the truth, and someone turns him back, let him know that he who turns a sinner from the error of his way will save a soul from death and cover a multitude of sins."

The church is a hospital for the sick, not a resort for the healthy. We are all ill with the disease of sin and need healing and restoration. Yet we find that some in the church think they have arrived and thus sit in judgment on the rest. They assume that they are whole and have a responsibility to safeguard their spiritual resort from contamination. Thus sometimes one does not even have to do something wrong to get ostracized. It only has to appear that way to this group, and someone is judged and purged from the body of believers. But that is not God's intent for the church or for His people.

Several years ago a member struggling to maintain his union with God found himself summoned outside from a large church function for arrest by the police, who charged him with raping a minor. Though his pastor and several church board members were there, no one accompanied him to the station, visited him, or called him. They shunned him as they would leprosy. Later that very evening they removed his name from membership, not wanting the newspapers to identify him with their congregation when reporting the incident.

Interestingly, after the police completed the investigation, they exonerated the man, because the charge had no truth to it. Yet he had been already ejected without due process—no interview, investigation, or hearing. One would naturally have expected them at least to apologize and reinstate him. But they treated him as a new member, giving no apology, expression of remorse, or regret for their tactless behavior. To make matters worse, at his reinstatement ceremony the pastor bellowed, "Brother Doe, this is your last chance." Such an action is contrary to the teaching of Scripture generally and the book of James particularly.

James begins with "brethren," again showing his love, care, and concern for fellow believers. His use of the term reinforces the idea that the church should be an accepting, loving, and caring community. No one is perfect, and but for God's grace everyone would be lost. I believe many harsh and unloving people don't love or respect themselves. It is therefore impossible for them to give to others what they don't have for themselves. Yet Jesus said—and we must practice—"By this all will know that you are My disciples, if you have love for one another" (John 13:35).

We need to explore several aspects of James 5:19, 20. First is the idea of wandering away from the truth. The second notion is "turning him back," something that I will label as restoration. The third concept is that of "saving a soul from death," what I will term salvation. The final element concerns "covering a multitude of sins."

Human beings are by nature inquisitive. It means we like to experiment and inspect things. That can sometimes lead us down unplanned paths and/or unexpected turns. Often we do not realize until too late that we have missed the path. I will use Jesus' teachings in four parables[1] in Luke 15 to illustrate four ways of wandering away from God and how we can reclaim those following such paths. The parables have common features—something is lost, then is found, and then the finding is celebrated. The fourth is an exception. It has the first two features but not the third.

Ways of Wandering Away

The parable of the lost sheep (Luke 15:4-7) illustrates the first way one can wander away from the community. Jesus tells the story in the active voice, not the passive. The passive would have suggested that the sheep got lost on its own accord. "What man of you, having a hundred sheep, if *he loses one* of them" (verse 4) implies that the sheep didn't just go astray. The active voice infers that the shepherd's neglect caused the loss. Not all those who have left the church did so of their own volition. Some were lost because of our neglect as shepherds and/or religious leaders—lay or clerical. Shepherds protect, care for, and are personally responsible for the sheep. If one is lost, hired shepherds[2] must show its fleece or pay for it from their wages.

The first way to be lost, then, is to be pushed out through neglect, slights, or other action on the part of leadership. Leaders must be alert to the needs of the flock and must attend to them. We also need to be sensitive to the idiosyncrasies of each sheep and endeavor not to wound or hurt them needlessly, but preserve them all for the kingdom. Jesus told the Father in prayer that He had kept all those given to Him except Judas (John 17:12; 18:9).

The second manner of becoming lost appears in Luke 15:8-10, the story of a silver coin. It is an interesting representation of one who wanders from the truth in that the coin is a thing. A Greek drachma (equivalent to a Roman denarius) represented a day's wage and thus was not much money. Yet, though a thing, it is silver, which means that it has intrinsic worth. All in God's flock, even those who wander away, have value. Many view this parable as a twin of the lost sheep, because they are alike in several aspects. The coin is a thing and therefore cannot wander away. Someone has to misplace or lose it. Like the first parable, Jesus here employs the active voice, again suggesting that it was the owner—the woman—who lost it. The parable is unique to Luke, whose emphasis is salvation. He wants it known that Jesus came to seek and to save the *lost*, especially outcasts, those on the fringes of society, and women. Thus the parable highlights a loss by one on the fringe of society—a woman.

Whereas the first parable features the loss by a man, this one involves a woman. Inclusive, Jesus resisted a society that discriminated against women. Thus He took a principled stance against its position and presented a woman here. God's church should also reject discrimination and other societal ills. Whereas the shepherd represents a leader or one in charge, the woman was not someone who was an authority.

The coin symbolizes those who are no longer in the fold through no fault of their own but may have been forced out by other members, whether through criticism, cynicism, ridicule, neglect, slights, or anything else. While we cannot justify their departure from the church, they represent a reality that we must not ignore or minimize. Members of God's flock have obligations for each other. We are our brothers' keepers. Scripture says that iron sharpens iron, which calls us to strengthen and encourage each other as we follow Jesus. Christians are not rivals or competitors. We complete, not compete with, each other.

The third parable (Luke 15:11-24) introduces a new twist. A human being replaces the animal and a lifeless coin as the thing lost. This loss, however, did not result from anybody's neglect or carelessness. Choosing his own destiny, the younger son made a deliberate decision to leave the fold. He went to his father, requested his portion of the estate, and deliberately wandered away.

For unknown reasons, he became dissatisfied with home and decided to leave. The story gives no evidence of prior discontent, yet such actions don't happen suddenly. Something must have been brewing. Knowing the ways of youth, we can surmise that he might have been unhappy with the supposed restrictions of home and thus longed for freedom. He seemed to have wanted his own way. That such could be the case we see evidenced by where he went and what he did upon leaving.

We notice an apparent arrogance in his attitude to his father. He demands his portion as if entitled to it. Yet no ancient Near Eastern law or custom authorized him a portion of his father's estate while his father lived. Ben Sirach said in 190 B.C., "To son or wife, to brother or friend, do not give power over yourself, as long as you live; and do not give your property to another, in case you change your mind and must ask for it. While you are still alive and have breath in you, do not let another take your place. . . . At the time when you end the days of your life, in the hour of death, distribute your inheritance" (Sirach 33:20-24, NRSV).

By requesting a portion before his father's death, he was really wishing his father dead. It was not only an improper demand but a great insult to his father. Yet the parable says the father accepted his request. The Greek says that he divided his *bion*—his life, his means of living, substance, or goods. As we have mentioned previously, people in those days did not convert property into cash, but always preserved it in the family.

Jewish teachers of the first century used the triadic form of presentation (presentations in groups of three) in their teaching. It may have influenced the format of Luke 15, as in the parable of the good Samaritan. But rather than a triad I see a quadriad here, and thus four rather than three parables—the fourth being that of the lost brother. If we regard the first two as twin parables, then the second two are also twins. While the first depicts an animate thing lost *away* from home, the second portrays an inanimate thing lost *in* the home. The third depicts a person lost away from home in contrast to the fourth, which describes a person lost in the home. And whereas the first parable exemplifies that the one lost knows its condition but cannot find the way back home, the second portrays something that is unaware of its state and does not know that it should return home. Finally, while the third depicts one who is lost, knows he is lost, and not only knows the way back home but actually makes that trek, the fourth may represent one who is lost, becomes aware of that fact, but chooses not to return. (The fate of the older brother remains open-ended, however.)

Essentially, then, in the four parables two losses occur away from home and two at home. An animal and a youth are lost away from home, while a lifeless object and a living person get lost at home. Not only are the parallels striking but the sequencing as well—away from home, at home; away from home, at home; also, dumb animal, inanimate object; responsive person and unresponsive person. All these factors help to substantiate the view that we do indeed find four parables here. Let's give the older brother his rightful place in the quadriad.

Thus the fourth parable depicts someone who is lost in the confines and safety of home. As the firstborn son, he had first dibs at his father's estate. Yet he felt he had nothing. His younger brother left home, squandered his substance, found the value of home, and returned to be a servant just to be near his father. Big brother never left home physically but did so psychologically, and, though a son, felt and acted like a servant. We see someone mired in a poor self-concept and causelessly wallowing in self-pity and an inferiority complex. He lived at home but had wandered away mentally, emotionally, and spiritually. Thus the fourth way of wandering away from the fold, then, is to do so mentally, emotionally, and spiritually while still being in it physically. No one pushes, slights, or wounds; no one is careless, indifferent, or thoughtless; no apparent dissatisfaction or discontent is evident; instead, there is only a drifting away in the mind, emotions, and spirit. The loss takes place in the eyes of everyone but unknown to anyone.

Restoration

The parables also contain insights on restoration. According to Middle Eastern custom, an individual shepherd would not own 100 sheep. One person usually possessed 5-15 sheep. A flock of 100 sheep would imply community ownership or an affluent owner with hired shepherds.[3] One shepherd wouldn't be alone with 100 sheep. It would require at least three shepherds for such a size flock.[4] What the shepherd does, on finding the sheep, intrigues me. It demonstrates the burdens of restoration. He joyfully places it on his shoulders and heads home. Why must he carry the sheep? I am told that a sheep lacks a sense of direction. When lost, it will lie helpless and won't move. The shepherd is thus forced to lift it physically and carry it long distances to safety.[5] Envision with me a shepherd hoisting a 100-pound sheep, placing it on his shoulders, and walking home with it. Please note that the shepherd does not blame, scold, correct, or spank the sheep. He joyfully puts it on his shoulders and takes it home.

It is an important point, because the sheep represents sinners who know they are lost but cannot find their way back home. We must go to look for them. At times we may even have to carry them. Moreover, Christians are hired shepherds who represent the Father. Our task is to tend His flock and care for His sheep. Therefore, notice how tender and compassionate He is—and thus how we must be! Notice also how the shepherd neither carries the sheep grudgingly nor blames it for wandering off. We too must joyfully restore the erring and those who have drifted away from the fold. The sheep is not only found but must be restored. Restoration involves the burden of carrying the sheep. Someone must willingly and joyfully bear that burden of saving sinners.

Luke depicts the shepherd as rejoicing twice. First, in the wilderness when he finds the sheep (Luke 15:5); and again, when he returns home. At this point he rejoices with the community (verse 6). The loss may have been a community one and thus the find a community occasion for rejoicing. All those who wander away from God are community losses, and there must be community joy and rejoicing to welcome them home. I am that sheep and so are you. We were lost from the fold, and someone turned us back and restored us. Let's do for others what was done for us. And let us do it with rejoicing.

The second parable tells something new about how restoration takes place. Not only must we go outside to find some wanderers, then lift and return them to the safety of the fold, but we must recognize that not all wanderers resemble or respond in similar ways, or understand truth in identical fashion. As an inanimate object, the coin does not know it is lost. Someone has to discover the loss, search for it, and then return it. Luke 15:8 says that the woman "lights a lamp, sweeps her house, and looks carefully everywhere." Contemporary readers often miss the impact of the story given our modern creature comforts. During the first century that floor would not have been a marble, slate, hardwood, or carpeted one. It was the dirt floor of a room with a small door and no window.[6] The woman must sweep the loose dirt from the floor to find the coin and do so carefully so as not to brush the coin away in the process. To accomplish her task effectively, the woman must light a lamp.

Finding a coin on a dirt floor is like searching for a needle in a haystack. But the woman had a mission and persisted. Though the undertaking was seemingly impossible, she undauntedly endured. We need the same attitude to reclaim wanderers from the kingdom. Breaking the habit of neglecting and blaming the lost and the straying, we must instead begin searching for them, inviting them back, and welcoming them home. The church must be a caring environment.

Today we view coins as cumbersome and prefer paper bills, checks, and credit cards. Twenty-one centuries ago people had no paper currency. They seldom had money, especially women. That fact made the loss an extremely sad and emotional event.[7] The coins were valuable to her. Perhaps they were her dowry. That she had the coins may suggest her husband had either died or had divorced her. In a society that determined a woman's value by her relationship to a man, the coins may have been her support for the rest of her life, for in that society women didn't work for pay as in ours. No wonder she lit the lamp and swept the floor.

Her diligence received its reward. She found the coin right there at home, i.e., the church. Some can even be lost while seeming to remain inside the church as members. What compounds the matter is the fact that the coin is a thing, which means it did not know it was lost and thus unaware of its need to find its way back home. That alludes to another aspect of restoration. Some, both in and out of the church, are unaware they are lost, oblivious of their condition, and indifferent about their future. Such individuals can't find the way back home. They need the gracious prodding or loving touch of someone to seek them out and make them aware of their true situation. And that takes love, patience, and compassion.

The parable gives a picture of a searching God. Yes, Jesus used a woman to represent the Father. That took moral courage, especially when speaking to the scribes and Pharisees. Again, He challenges their attitudes and rejects their dismissal of certain groups in society. Having come to seek and to save the lost, not reject them, He did not hesitate to challenge and reject the status quo and to stand for right, even if He was the only one. It required a good self-concept, moral courage, and a principled stance. I invite you to join Jesus on such issues. Stand for right! Reject the status quo when it conflicts with morality, justice, and right! Join Him in restoring people.

By taking his portion, the younger son gave up all rights or further claims to his father's estate and alienated himself from family. Away from the shelter of home and the watchful eyes of parents, he mismanaged his estate, wasting his substance in extravagant living. "He squandered his wealth" (Luke 15:13, NIV). Although apparently enjoying life, he had no concept of its responsibilities and demands and soon lost all he had, with no hope of regaining it.

Now he faced the dilemma of what to do. But having severed all ties with home and having lost everything, he had nowhere to go. When he had cash, he had friends. Without it, they forsook him. Deserted by friends, he had sunk into poverty. Desperate, he took work that was degrading for anyone but an atrocity for a Jew—feeding pigs for Gentiles. One rabbi said, "Cursed is he who feeds swine."[8] Here was a Jew not only hiring himself out as a pig herder, but competing with the animals themselves for food. Once having everything, he now had nothing. He suffered total rejection for "no one gave him anything" (verse 16). That is what sin does to people. It promises everything, delivers nothing, and leaves its captive in total rejection.

In the mire of the pigpen, something good happened: "He came to himself" (verse 17). The son remembered who he was and whose he was. Self-inventory led to an acknowledgment of his present state and ultimately a change of mind. We call it repentance. Yet repentance cannot take place where there is no sense of need and recognition of one's true condition. The prodigal came to himself and saw what he was missing—home. Furthermore, he grasped that even a slave at home lived better than he did—a little experience teaches a lot. Having reconciled himself to his past, he felt the need for restoration. That's the Spirit's work. As he came to himself he saw that he must be restored to the fellowship and warmth of home. Yet he knew that, while desirable, restoration carries obligations and has demands.

The prodigal decided to return home and face those demands. To do so, he prepared a well-thought-out speech (Luke 15:17-20). Let's analyze it. *Father*—he had humbled himself. Seeing his father in a new light, he was now willing to acknowledge him as a good father. *I have sinned*—he confessed his guilt and sin. *I am no longer worthy*—this reflects contrition. *To be called your son*—an acceptance of his true condition. *Make me like a hired servant*—his request/petition, knowing he had no more rights or privileges, having surrendered them with his insensitive and unreasonable demand. The son then made his way home, rehearsing his planned speech. Here we have the picture of those who know that they are lost and not only can find but make their way home. They feel the need for restoration and effect it under the conviction of the Holy Spirit.

E. E. Cleveland told a story about a girl named Mary Jones. During church service someone announced, "Mary Jones, if you are in the audience, please identify yourself to an usher. The police are looking for you, since you are reported lost." No one moved, so the service went on. At its conclusion a girl approached the pastor and said, "Sir, I am Mary Jones."

"Mary, what are you doing here? Don't you know that you are lost?"

"Sir, I am not lost," she replied. "I was just sitting in church."

The truth is many are lost just sitting in church. Was this true of the elder son?

His story is tragic. He had toiled in the fields all day and every day. On his way home, tired and hungry, he heard celebratory music in the house but knew of no scheduled event. Instantly he felt slighted. Instead of letting his father tell him what was happening, he asked a servant, who explained, "Your brother has come, and because he has received him safe and sound, your father has killed the fatted calf" (verse 27). The news embittered him and made him angry. After all, he had slaved at home, but his father had never done anything special for him. Now he refused to join the celebration, remaining outside. Although he too needed restoration, he did not know it.

But the father recognized that fact. Leaving the party, he went to meet the older son and to restore him. The older brother rebuffed him by never once addressing him as father. Note what his father said: "You are always with me, and everything I have is yours." But the son did not hear or accept that. He was so focused on his supposed hurt that he could not be reasoned with or be rational. The older brother took for granted what he had and coveted what his brother got. It's a sad state to be in. Sometimes we become so blinded by our own perspective that we lose sight of the big picture and—most notably—the divine perspective.

The contrast between the two sons is striking. The younger one left home to get freedom and lost what he had. The older brother had freedom at home and lost it through not knowing what he had. The younger claimed his rights but lost his relationships. The older diminished his bond while standing for his rights. The younger came to himself, desired his relationships, and went home seeking them. The older stood for his rights and destroyed the relationships. While the younger always addressed his dad as "father," the older son refused to address him as such.

The younger son returned home wishing to be regarded as a servant if only he could have the joy, happiness, and fellowship of home again. The older son devalued home, refused to act like a son, behaved like a slave, and lost happiness at home. The younger son got lost away from home, while the older son became lost at home—lost in church. Regrettably, the parable does not state that he was restored. It leaves him out in the cold in anger and rage. Yet how could he be restored if he felt no need for renewal and didn't request it? The same is true of some older brothers in our churches today. They sit judgmentally on others, not knowing their own true need of restoration. Let's not forget that the father waited patiently for the return of his son. So should we!

Salvation

Each parable features someone playing the role of turning the wanderer from error—the shepherd, the woman, the younger brother himself, and the father. James says the person who performs the role will save a soul. Unfortunately, some do the opposite, as we see illustrated in the fourth parable. The servant does not help in restoring a wanderer. Rather, like some in the church, they provide accurate information but with wrong timing or inappropriate slants.

Also, the father pleaded with the older brother, but the son insulted him and remained in the dark of anger, jealousy, and despair. He criticized his father and refused the love the father gave him. While he demanded his rights he failed to value his relationships and couldn't identify with the rebirth of his brother. Turning a sinner from error and saving a soul were irrelevant to him. The older brother did not want to cover a multitude of evil. The restoration of the younger brother puzzled him, the celebration of his return distressed him, and his father's forgiveness annoyed him. Some in the church still respond in the same way. It is puzzling how the ones at home, in the safety of the fold, can react so indifferently and callously to the restoration of the lost. Hostile, the older brother could not identify with his sibling, just as some in the church can't rejoice with new believers. "This son of yours who has squandered your property" (verse 30, NIV), he tells his father. Notice that it is "your son," not even "my brother."

Another amazing reality concerns how the older son and some Christians go through life without evaluating their positions and learning to appreciate their blessings. The older brother was always at home. All that his father had was his. Yet he didn't value what he had—neither his father nor his blessings. It wasn't until his younger brother was restored that he took any thought but with the wrong approach. Rather than eliciting gratitude, it sparked jealousy and self-pity. Instead of self-examination and reflection, he compared himself with his brother and concluded that the brother was ahead of him. Wrongly deciding that his father gave his undeserving brother more than he did him, he became envious and then jealous. Jealousy led to hatred and hatred to bitterness. He was lost at home, and where is home? The church.

Many sit in church each week but neither value God nor their fellow human being. They do not appreciate the blessings the Lord gives us each day—health, strength, life, family, jobs, Christian brothers and sisters. Instead, they compare themselves with others and conclude that God loves those others more than them. They then become envious and jealous, leading them to hate, malign, misrepresent, tear down, and destroy their fellow brothers and sisters, when the problem is with them and their attitude. Do you know that self is at the root of all sin? Let's check it out. To envy or be jealous of another, we must first compare ourselves with others and conclude that they have somehow gotten ahead of us. This leads to the "me and you," "us and them" relationship exhibited by the older son. Many envy the blessings that others get when they exercise big faith when the problem is with their own small faith. Remember that Jesus said, "According to your faith let it be to you" (Matt. 9:29).

The older son's first problem was his lack of appreciation for what he had. That led to estrangement from those he loved. His next mistake was to contrast himself with his brother. God does not expect us to compare ourselves with anything or anyone but Jesus. Fix your gaze on Him. Behold the splendor and majesty of His wonderful face, and you will begin to see things in their right perspective.

While the lost coin is a twin to the lost sheep, we also find affinities and parallels between the lost coin and the older brother. The coin was lost at home but did not know it was lost and thus could not find its way home. The older brother too was lost at home, knew he was lost, could find his way home, and was even offered support, as the coin got, but apparently refused any assistance for restoration to fellowship. It is impossible to help anyone who does not feel the need for restoration or want it.

Before moving on, we should explore another common feature illustrating what our attitudes to restoration should be. The shepherd rejoices twice on finding the lost sheep—once in the wilderness and again in the community. The woman calls her friends and neighbors and has them rejoice with her on finding the lost coin. The father not only rejoices on finding his son, but throws a party with celebration. Then the father goes out and invites his older son to join the party and rejoice, but the son rejects the offer. The reclaiming of sinners should always lead to rejoicing. Luke 15:7 tells us heaven celebrates even one sinner who repents and is restored. If that is the attitude in heaven, what should be ours on earth? There should be rejoicing too! Let us restore the lost and let us rejoice and celebrate with them. Baptism and accession services are opportunities for happiness and celebration. Let's do on earth what heaven does to welcome new entrants to the kingdom of God!

Finally, how does one cover a multitude of evil? David declares in Psalm 32:1: "Blessed is he whose transgression is forgiven, whose sin is covered." It says forgiveness covers our sins. When we find someone who has strayed from the fold, when we restore them from error and introduce them to God and He saves them, they are in a new space. God justifies them by forgiving their sins and casting them into the depths of the sea (Micah 7:19). A hospitalized patient who spent his time reading his Bible would every so often shout, "Amen! Praise the Lord! Hallelujah!" It began to annoy some staff members. They took away his Bible and gave him a geography book, hoping to silence him. Soon they again heard him shouting, "Amen! Praise the Lord! Hallelujah!" Stunned, they ran to him said, "We took your Bible and gave you a geography book. What can you find in it to be shouting about?"

"When I read the Bible, it says God will cast my sins into the depths of the sea. And when I read this book, it says the deepest part of the sea is seven miles. This says God will cover my sins with seven miles of water. Isn't that something to shout about?" Forgiven sins are covered not only with water, but with Jesus' blood. The greatest news is that He'll now view forgiven sinners as though they had never sinned. While it is an awesome thought, more important, it is a remarkable reality to experience.

A second way to cover a multitude of evil is through love. Proverbs says, "Hatred stirs up strife, but love covers all sins" (Prov. 10:12). To expose the sins of others, then, reveals a lack of love. When we genuinely love, we will protect each other, for love covers all sins. Another powerful passage makes the point even more emphatically: "And above all things have fervent love for one another, for 'love will cover a multitude of sins'"

(1 Peter 4:8). The NIV says we must have deep love for one another. The NRSV labels it "constant" love. The love here is agape love—a benevolent, nongrasping love that has the best interest of the one loved in view. It loves not for what it can get but for what it can give—for what another can become. When Christians love each other deeply, constantly, sincerely, they will defend, not expose, each other. We don't cut off a bad finger—we dress and protect it until it heals. It is in this way that we should treat a brother or a sister who falls into sin. When we do, we allow love to cover a multitude of evil, as James admonishes.

Application

James's final message is extremely relevant for us in the twenty-first century. We divide ourselves into camps and take positions that separate and fragment God's people to the extent that some don't see others as brothers and sisters. That is wrong! Maybe it is one way that we have wandered away from the truth, because we have made nonmoral issues more important than moral ones and have allowed them to distort Jesus to the world. You may ask how. As we have seen, prior to His departure Jesus said, "A new commandment I give unto you, That ye love one another; as I have loved you, that ye also love one another. By this shall all men know that ye are my disciples, if ye have love one to another" (John 13:34, 35, KJV). When we fragment and divide Christ's body, aren't we thereby not exhibiting love and therefore misrepresenting Him?

Such love and inclusiveness manifests itself in still another way. Many today see truth as something we do and know rather than something to be. In other words, we treat truth as abstract knowledge rather than tenets to incorporate into our daily lives. Yet if the truth we know and love does not become a part of who we are, it can't modify our behavior and guide our lives. It is more important to be truthful than to know truth; to experience and reciprocate love than to know about love; to experience and give forgiveness than to merely know what forgiveness is.

Could it be that an approach to Christianity and the gospel regarding it as something to know and do will make us at times oblivious to the way we treat each other? The judgmental, harsh, and critical attitudes that some display will wound others and cause them to wander away. In some places we find cliques based on language, race, ethnicity, dialect, place of origin, and even eye color that include some and exclude others. They also contribute to divisions that drive some people away.

A sincere Christian became the chair of the board of elders at his church. The congregation did not believe in eating meat, and neither did he and his family. However, his wife became ill, and her doctor recommended that because of the nature of her illness she should begin to eat meat again. Desiring to regain her health, she did so. Her husband joined her at times. Soon some of the church members heard that they were eating meat. No one spoke directly to them or tried to find out why they were eating it. Fellow believers began to shun them and talk about them behind their backs. The criticism got so severe and so harsh that the couple discontinued fellowship with them and wandered away from God.

Another time a woman responded to a call to join the church. When she got up front, it produced a noticeable reaction from everyone. Later some members went to the pastor to object, saying, "You don't know her. We do. She has a dishonorable reputation and is at odds with most people in the community. We recommend that you don't accept her." The pastor called a meeting to discuss the issue. They came united against her. At the last moment one member relented and suggested it would be good to invite her to discuss the issue before voting. At the meeting, before anyone could ask a question, she said, "I know the seriousness of what I am undertaking. I have found and love Jesus. Therefore, I have been through the community and have made it right with everyone whether I had a problem with them or them with me. I am now ready to proceed." Everyone was speechless. They had all learned a valuable lesson that day.

The harsh critical voices of some members could have forever wounded her. But the individual who spoke up at the first meeting saved a soul. While we should not condone sin, we must allow the blood of Christ to cover a multitude of evil. We do so by being kind, tolerant, compassionate, understanding, loving, forgiving, and long-suffering. That is how God is to us and how we should be to others. What if we make deliberate efforts to reclaim former members who have been lost as a result of the use of wrong methods? What if we go even further and establish ministries to accomplish the task? God will be pleased. And what is stopping us from beginning? Will you make a promise to God right now to do something to start reclaiming the lost?

---

[1] Most commentators speak of three parables and subsume the fourth in the third. Bailey sees the third parable as consisting of two parts with the same message (see Kenneth E. Bailey, *Poet and Peasant: A Literary-Cultural Approach to the Parables of Luke*

[Grand Rapids: Wm. B. Eerdmans, 1976], pp. 190, 200, 201). I will separate them out and demonstrate that the fourth has its own message that we can miss when we submerge into the third parable.

[2] In biblical times there were both owner shepherds and hired ones. The shepherding cycle was seven years. That is why Jacob had to work 14 years for his two wives. The hired shepherds' pay came from the number of sheep above the agreed-upon number that would be returned at the end of the cycle. Lost sheep came from his wages unless he could prove, usually by the fleece, that wild beasts had devoured them.

[3] Bailey, p. 148.

[4] *Ibid.*

[5] *Ibid.*

[6] Cf. William Barclay, *The Gospel of Luke,* rev. ed. (Philadelphia: Westminster Press, 1975), p. 202; A. T. Robertson, *Word Pictures,* vol. 2, p. 207.

[7] Bailey, p. 157.

[8] See, among others, Leon Morris, *The Gospel According to St. Luke,* Tyndale New Testament Commentaries (Grand Rapids: Wm. B. Eerdmans, 1979), p. 241.

Conclusion

At the outset I promised you a fascinating encounter with the book of James. I endeavored to make it as interesting and as provocative as possible. We trust that you experienced it that way. But we hope it was more than that. May James speak to you as powerfully and profoundly as he did to his first readers. Indeed, I hope that you succeeded in revitalizing your relationship with Jesus, thus breaking the stranglehold of desire and thereby sin's reign over you. Moreover, we hope James succeeded in challenging you to recognize that you are broken and that Jesus wants you to be whole. If you succeeded in this, you have been able to attain that Christian integrity in which belief leads to a changed life. Yet all this is not a goal or a destination. It is a daily walk with God that must be renewed and accomplished every day that we live in a sinful body and in a sinful environment.

Why did James spend so much time talking about the tongue? Because it is a major organ of speech, and it is our word that makes us Christians of integrity. We need to keep our word, and when we can't, we must still honor it. Here is one—if not the greatest—avenue of evangelism. We trust that reading this work has helped you to consider and practice discipleship of the tongue, pocketbook, and mind seriously. If you are still not convinced on a number of the items James advocates, don't reject them. Try them on and see if they fit you. You might be surprised to discover what the Holy Spirit might do with them in your life.

Being a Christian is not just about knowing doctrines, going to church, or working for those already in the church. While all this and more, it is experiencing the love of God; allowing it to become a way of life; letting it effect change in your life; and having done so, reaching back to bestow it on another and thereby help liberate someone traveling behind us. So build bridges of love, hope, understanding, justice, and peace. Then bring others across from error to experience the awesome acceptance and love of a God who will cover a multitude of evil with the blood of Christ.

Finally, don't just read the book of James and put it down, as we do others. It is a book to be lived. Welcome to a new world of encounter. And, don't forget, we are in it together. We are in the same struggle, and can have the same victory—victory in Christ.

Selection From Ellen G. White, Spiritual Gifts, vol. 2, pp. 184-188.

And I was constantly afflicted with the thought that my eye might be destroyed with a cancer. I looked back to the days and nights spent in reading proof-sheets, which had strained my eyes, and thought if I lose my eye, and my life, it will be a martyr to the cause.

A celebrated physician visited Rochester who gave counsel free. I decided to have him examine my eye. He thought the swelling would prove to be a cancer. He felt my pulse, and said, "You are much diseased, and will die of apoplexy before that swelling will break out. You are in a dangerous condition with disease of the heart." This did not startle me, for I had been aware that unless I received speedy relief I must lie in the grave. Two other females had come for counsel who were suffering with the same disease. The physician said that I was in a more dangerous condition than either of them, and it could not be more than three weeks before I would be afflicted with paralysis, and next would follow apoplexy. I inquired if he thought his medicine would cure me. He did not give me much encouragement. I purchased some of his medicine. The eyewash was very painful, and I received no benefit from it. I was unable to use the remedies the physician prescribed.

In about three weeks I fainted and fell to the floor, and remained unconscious about thirty-six hours. It was feared that I could not live; but in answer to prayer again I revived. One week later, while conversing with sister Anna, I received a shock upon my left side. My head was numb, I had a strange sensation of coldness and numbness in my head, with pressure, and severe pain through my temples. My tongue seemed heavy and numb. I could not speak plainly. My left arm and side were helpless. I thought I was dying, and my great anxiety was to have the evidence amid my suffering that the Lord loved me. . . .

The brethren and sisters came together to make my case a special subject of prayer. My desire was granted. Prayer was heard, and I received the blessing of God, and had the assurance that He loved me. But the pain continued, and I grew more feeble every hour. The brethren and sisters again came together to present my case to the Lord. I was then so weak that I could not pray vocally. My appearance seemed to weaken the faith of those around me. Then the promises of God were arrayed before me as I had never viewed them before. It seemed to me that Satan was striving to tear me from my husband and children, and lay me in the grave, and these questions were suggested to my mind, Can you believe the naked promises of God? Can ye walk out by faith, let the appearances be what they may? Faith revived. I whispered to my husband, I believe that I shall recover. He answered, "I wish I could believe it." I retired that night without relief, yet relying with firm confidence upon the promises of God. I could not sleep, but continued my silent prayer to God. Just before day I slept. As I awoke, the sun was seen from my window, arising in the east. I was perfectly free from pain. The pressure and weight upon my heart was gone, and I was very happy. I was filled with gratitude. The praise of God was upon my lips. O what a change! It seemed to me that an angel of God had touched me while I was sleeping. I awoke my husband and related to him the wonderful work that the Lord had wrought for me. He could scarcely comprehend it at first. But when I arose and dressed, and walked around the house, and he witnessed the change in my countenance, he could praise God with me. My afflicted eye was free from pain. In a few days I looked in the glass, the cancer was gone, and my eyesight was fully restored. The work was complete.

Again I visited the physician, and as soon as he felt my pulse he said, "Madam, you are better. An entire change has taken place in your system; but the two women who visited me for counsel when you were last here are dead." I told him it was not his medicine that had cured me, for I could use none of it. . . . Sister P., who now rests in the grave, had accompanied me, and related to the physician after I left, that the Lord had heard prayer for me, and restored me to health. Said he, "Her case is a mystery. I do not understand it."

Bibliography

Arndt, William, and F. Wilbur Gingrich. *A Greek-English Lexicon of the New Testament*. Chicago: University of Chicago Press, 1959.

Bailey, Kenneth E. *Poet and Peasant: A Literary-Cultural Approach to the Parables in Luke*. Grand Rapids: Wm. B. Eerdmans, 1976.

Barclay, William. *The Letters to the Corinthians*. Rev. ed. Philadelphia: Westminster Press, 1975.

Blount, Brian K., gen. ed. *True to Our Native Land: An African American New Testament Commentary*. Minneapolis: Fortress Press, 2007.

Davids, Peter H. *The Epistle of James: A Commentary on the Greek Text*. Online ed. Grand Rapids: Wm. B. Eerdmans, 1982.

Ellsworth, Roger. *James*. Leominster, Mass.: Day One Publications, 2009.

Elwell, Walter A., and Philip Wesley Comfort. *Tyndale Bible Dictionary*. Tyndale Reference Library. Wheaton, Ill.: Tyndale House Publishers, 2001.

Freedman, David Noel, ed. *The Anchor Bible Dictionary*. New York: Doubleday, 1992. 6 vols.

Horn, Siegfried H. *Seventh-day Adventist Bible Dictionary*. Rev. ed. Washington, D.C.: Review and Herald, 1979.

Keener, Craig S. *The IVP Bible Background Commentary: New Testament*. Downers Grove, Ill.: InterVarsity Academic Press, 1993.

King, Martin Luther, Jr. "Letter From Birmingham Jail," Apr. 16, 1963.

Kittel, Gerhard, and Gerhard Friedrich, eds. *Theological Dictionary of the New Testament*. Grand Rapids: Wm. B. Eerdmans, 1964-1976. 10 vols.

Kümmel, Werner G. *Introduction to the New Testament*. Trans. Howard Clark Kee. Rev. English ed. Nashville: Abingdon Press, 1975.

Loh, I-Jin, and Howard A. Hatton. *A Translator's Handbook on the Letter From James*. Online ed. New York: United Bible Societies, 1997.

Longenecker, Richard, ed. *Patterns of Discipleship in the New Testament.* Grand Rapids: Wm. B. Eerdmans, 1996.

Martin, Ralph P., and Peter H. Davids, eds. *Dictionary of the Later New Testament and Its Developments.* Downers Grove, Ill.: InterVarsity Press, 1997.

———. *James. Word Biblical Commentary.*Waco, Tex.: Word Books, 1988.

Mayor, Joseph P. *The Epistle of St. James.* Online ed.

Melbourne, Bertram L. *Slow to Understand: The Disciples in Synoptic Perspective.* Lanham, Md.: University Press of America, 1988.

Metzger, Bruce. *The New Testament: Its Background, Growth, and Content.* Nashville: Abingdon, 1982.

Moo, Douglas J. *The Letter of James, The Pillar New Testament Commentary.* Online ed. Grand Rapids: Wm. B. Eerdmans Publishing Company, 2000.

Morris, Leon. *The Gospel According to St. Luke. Tyndale New Testament Commentaries.* Grand Rapids: Wm. B. Eerdmans, 1979.

Nasby, Gordon A., ed. *Treasury of the Christian World.* New York: Harper and Brothers, 1953.

Nichol, Francis D., ed. *The Seventh-day Adventist Bible Commentary.* Hagerstown, Md.: Review and Herald Publishing Association, 1980. 7 vols.

Richardson, Kurt A. *James.* Logos Library System. The New American Commentary. Electronic ed. Nashville: Broadman and Holman Publishers, 2001.

Robertson, A. T. *Word Pictures in the New Testament.* Grand Rapids: Baker Book House, 1930. 6 vols.

Tomlinson, Gerald. *Treasury of Religious Quotations.* Eaglewood Cliffs, N.J.: Prentice Hall, 199_.

White, Ellen. G. *The Desire of Ages.* Mountain View, Calif.: Pacific Press Publishing Association. 1898.

———. *Fundamentals of Christian Education.* Nashville: Southern Publishing Association, 1923.

———. *Gospel Workers.* Washington, D.C.: Review and Herald Publishing Association, 1915.

———. *Messages to Young People.* Washington, D.C.: Review and Herald Publishing Association, 1930.

———. *Steps to Christ.* Mountain View, Calif.: Pacific Press Publishing Association, 1956.

———. *Spiritual Gifts.* Battle Creek, Mich.: Seventh-day Adventist Publishing Association, 1858, 1860, 1864. 4 vols.

———. *Testimonies for the Church*. Mountain View, Calif.: Pacific Press
Publishing Association, 1948. 9 vols.

———. *Thoughts From the Mount of Blessing*. Mountain View, Calif.: Pacific
Press Publishing Association, 1956.

Wiersbe, Warren W. *The Bible Expository Commentary*. Wheaton, Ill.: Victory Books, 1989.

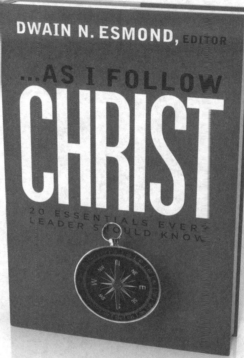

This Could Change Everything

Find transforming power for your life

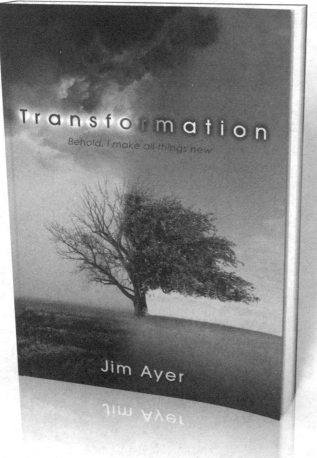

They Didn't Believe in Jesus.

He Showed Up Anyway.

"WHAT IS THE TRUTH ABOUT JESUS? WAS HE MORE THAN JUST A CARPENTER FROM NAZARETH? MORE THAN ANOTHER GREAT TEACHER? EXAMINE THE RADICAL EVIDENCE FOR YOURSELF."
—Josh McDowell, author of More Than a Carpenter

Radical Evidence
Derek J. Morris

In his latest book, Derek Morris introduces you to people who have had a dramatic encounter with the Messiah they didn't believe in. There's a Shiite Muslim and an African ancestor worshipper. There's Clifford Goldstein, an atheist and obsessed novelist who found his life taking an unexpected turn.

People in Bible times also present evidence. There are the prophets who spoke of things they did not understand, but whose words came true in the gospel story.

Perhaps you have a friend who has doubts about the divinity of Jesus. Or maybe you work with a straight-up unbeliever. Invite them to read this book and see the radical evidence for a real and personal Savior.

Hardcover: 973-0-8127-0514-0.

DVD: Four presentations, approx. 28 minutes each. 978-1-936929-07-8.

Other books in the Radical series you may enjoy

THE RADICAL PRAYER

Hardcover
978-0-8127-0486-0

Audio CD
978-0-981712-41-3

DVD
978-0-981712-40-6

Spanish Paperback
978-8-472082-67-0

RADICAL PROTECTION

Hardcover
978-0-8127-0476-1

Audio CD
978-1-936929-01-6

DVD
978-1-936929-00-9

Trilogy Scripture Songs CD
978-1-936929-02-3

THE RADICAL TEACHINGS OF JESUS

Hardcover
978-0-8127-0498-3

Audio CD
978-0-981712-49-9

DVD
978-0-981712-42-0

Leader's Kit
978-1-932267-77-8

Price and availability subject to change.